Leonardo da Vinci for Kids

Leonardo da Vinci

HIS LIFE AND IDEAS 21 ACTIVITIES

Kids

Janis Herbert

CHICAGO REVIEW PRESS

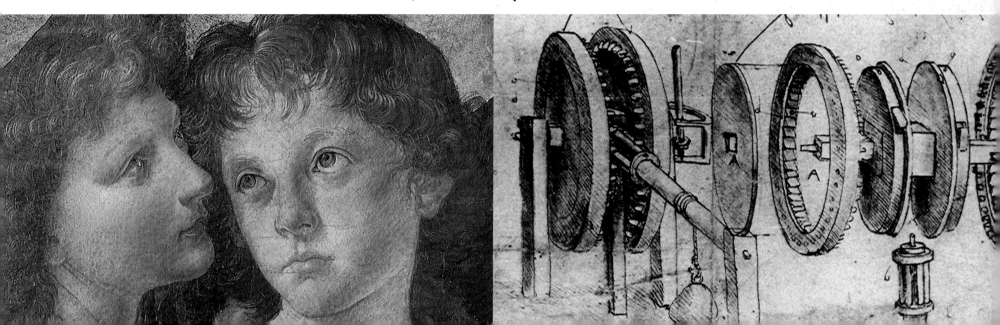

© 1998 by Janis Herbert

First edition
Published by Chicago Review Press, Incorporated
814 North Franklin Street
Chicago, Illinois 60610

ISBN 978-1-55652-298-7

10 9 8 7 6

Cover design: Sean O'Neill
Cover art courtesy of Wood River Gallery
Interior design: Joan Sommers Design

Printed in Singapore by CS Graphics

Library of Congress Cataloging-in-Publication Data

Herbert, Janis, 1956–
    Leonardo da Vinci for kids : his life and ideas : 21 activities /
Janis Herbert. — 1st ed.
        p.   cm.
    Includes bibliographical references.
    Summary : Presents a biography of this prolific artist and
inventor through projects in cartography, animal art, bird observation, and mask making.
    1. Leonardo, da Vinci, 1452–1519—Juvenile literature.
2. Artists—Italy—Biography—Juvenile literature. 3. Creative
activities and seat work—Juvenile literature. [1. Leonardo, da
Vinci, 1452-1519. 2. Artists. 3. Handicraft.] I. Title.
N6923.L33H47   1998
709'.2-dc21
[b]   98-25690
                                                          CIP
                                                           AC

To Jeff

CONTENTS

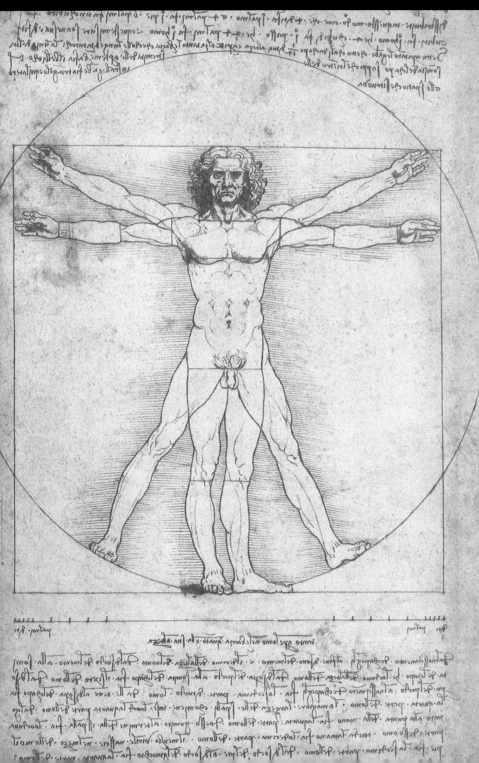

Acknowledgments   viii

Note to Readers   ix

Timeline   x

ONE A Boy in Vinci   1

Setting Up Your Studio   2

Observing Nature   3

Brush Up on Birds   4

TWO The Young Apprentice   7

A Beaker for Brushes   8

Framed!   10

A Life Mask   13

Kitchen Clay   15

Perspective   16

The Renaissance   18

Animal Art   20

Well-Bannered   25

Pinpointing the Vanishing Point   27

THREE   # A Genius at Work   29

Leonardo's Letter to Ludovico   30

Leonardo's Lute   31

Mirror Writing   32

A Discovery Notebook   33

Measuring Up   35

The Plague   38

A Masque of the Planets   40

Leonardo's Prophecies   41

Eye Exercises   42

Leonardo's Inventions   43

Italy's Kingdoms and
   City-States   44

Leonardo's Lunch   46

For the Birds   47

Salai's Aniseed Sweets   49

Mental Exercise   50

Leonardo's Lock   51

Learn a Little Italian   52

Flight   54

A Parachute Kite   55

Restoring *The Last Supper*   58

Missiles and Math   60

FOUR   # "I Shall Continue."   61

The Nature of Sound   63

Art Detectives   64

The Craft of Cartography   65

How Tall Is That Tree?   66

Simple Machines   68

Who Was Mona Lisa?   70

Looking at Art   72

A Renaissance Herb Garden   77

Glossary   80

Biographies   82

Resources   85

Bibliography   87

Credits   88

Left: Diagram of
human proportions,
Leonardo da Vinci,
1492

ACKNOWLEDGMENTS

Thanks to Rick Dissen and Andreas Mueller for their contributions to this work and to Sara Dickinson and Camillo Imbimbo for their advice and support. Many thanks to Joan Sommers for her design work, which beautifully reflects the spirit of the great artist Leonardo. I am grateful for the help of my resourceful mother, Ruth Ross; Cynthia Sherry, the most helpful of editors; talented cover designer Sean O'Neill; and, most of all, my wonderful husband, Jeff. With thanks and love to you all.

See the glossary on page 80 for an explanation of terms used in this book that you may be unfamiliar with. In the biography section beginning on page 82, you will find additional information about historical figures and Renaissance artists who are referred to in the book. There is also a resource section on page 86 that lists interesting web sites related to da Vinci and his interests, and museums around the world where you can see his paintings.

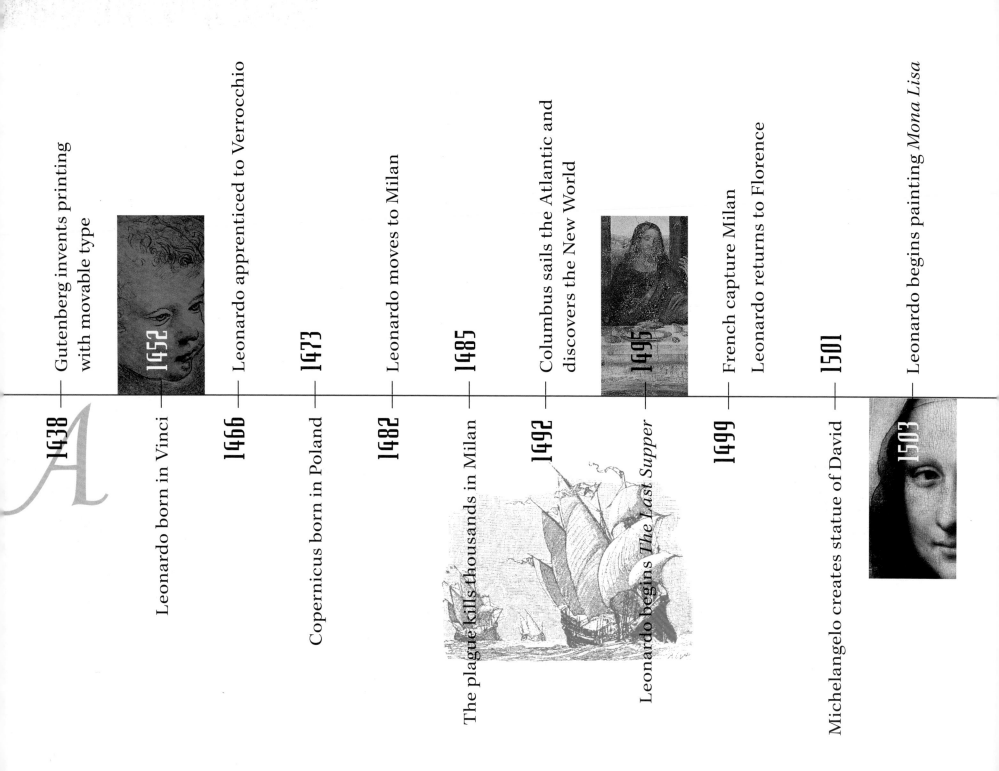

1438 Gutenberg invents printing with movable type

1452 Leonardo born in Vinci

1466 Leonardo apprenticed to Verrocchio

1473 Copernicus born in Poland

1482 Leonardo moves to Milan

1485 The plague kills thousands in Milan

1492 Columbus sails the Atlantic and discovers the New World

1495 Leonardo begins *The Last Supper*

1499 French capture Milan

Leonardo returns to Florence

1501 Michelangelo creates statue of David

1503 Leonardo begins painting *Mona Lisa*

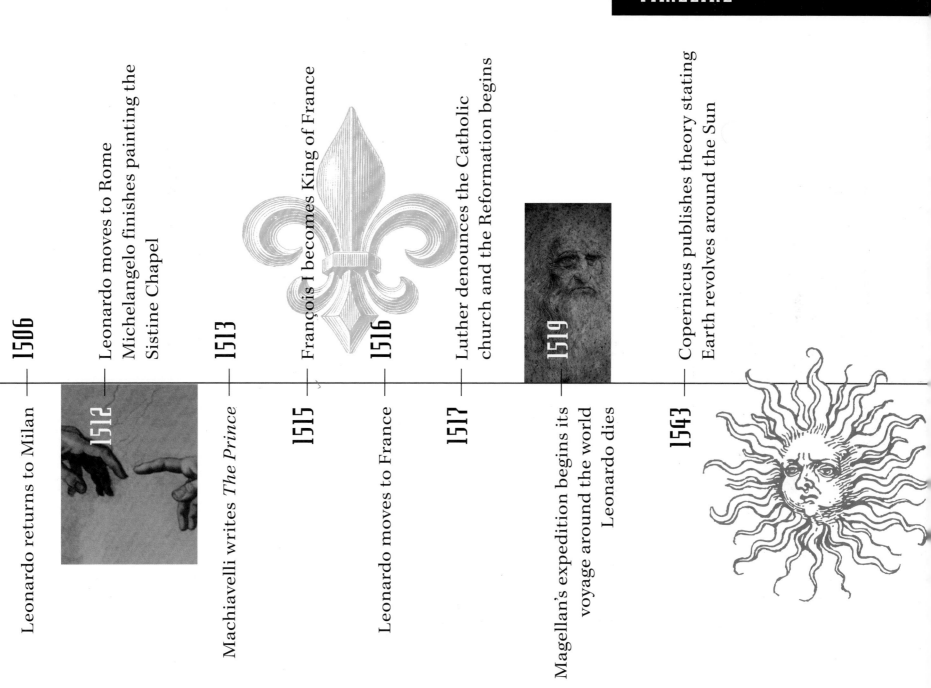

1506
Leonardo returns to Milan

1512
Leonardo moves to Rome
Michelangelo finishes painting the Sistine Chapel

1513
Machiavelli writes *The Prince*

1515
François I becomes King of France

1516
Leonardo moves to France

1517
Luther denounces the Catholic church and the Reformation begins

1519
Magellan's expedition begins its voyage around the world
Leonardo dies

1543
Copernicus publishes theory stating Earth revolves around the Sun

ONE

A Boy in Vinci

The baby's mother rushed out to the yard, waving her arms. A hawk was perched on her child's cradle. "Shoo!" she cried. The bird lifted its wings and flew off. For a moment she thought it would grasp the baby in its claws to carry him away over the hills—but the child was safe. When she reached down to pick him up, he was following the hawk's flight with his eyes and smiling.

The child, Leonardo, was born on April 15, 1452, in a mountainous region of Italy called Tuscany, near the small village of Vinci. His mother, Caterina, was a young peasant woman, beautiful and poor. His father, Ser Piero, was an ambitious young man from a wealthy family, who was just beginning his career as a notary. Leonardo's parents did not marry each other. As a baby, Leonardo stayed with his mother. When he was almost two years old he was taken from her home and raised on his father's estate.

Ser Piero was often away on business, traveling to neighboring towns. Eventually he met and married a young, wealthy woman, Albiera di Giovanni Amadori, and they settled in her home in the city of Florence. It was decided that Leonardo would remain in Vinci, and he was raised by his grandparents and his uncle Francesco.

Uncle Francesco was only sixteen years older than Leonardo. Though he was young, he ran the family estate. He supervised the work in the fields, where they raised olives, grapes, and wheat. Leonardo adored his uncle and

Left: Study for the head of Leda, Leonardo da Vinci, 1505–07

Right: Detail from Study for a Madonna and Child, Leonardo da Vinci, 1478

Painting is born of nature. —Leonardo

Set up a special place in your home for art projects. Here's what you might keep there.

Paper There are many types of paper, all made for different uses. For writing and sketching you can buy a sketch pad at an art supply store or make your own sketching notebook (see page 33). Special absorbent paper is made for watercolor painting, but construction paper also works well. Try different kinds of papers for painting and see what suits you best. Just be sure it's not shiny—shiny paper won't absorb paint. Canvas pads are available for painting with oils and acrylics. Keep a supply of different colored construction paper available for art projects.

Pencils and Erasers Graphite drawing pencils are graded with numbers and letters. They range from "10H" (which is a very hard pencil) to "10B" (a very soft one). A good pencil to start with is "HB." This pencil can make both strong dark lines and more delicate lines. Experiment with different grades of pencils from an art supply store. While you're there, buy a couple of erasers. A kneaded eraser is handy. It can be formed into any shape you need for erasing pencil marks. A pencil sharpener is also a necessary item.

Paints Experiment with different types—such as watercolor, tempera, acrylic, and oil—and start with a few basic colors. Each type of paint has a different quality that requires different techniques. Over time you might discover you prefer one type over another. Many paints come in starter sets. By mixing colors together you can make additional colors.

Paintbrushes Brushes also come in many sizes and types. Again, you might want to try several different kinds to find out what you like best. There are round brushes and flat ones, brushes for fine work and for broad strokes. The numbers on brushes indicate their size (the higher the number, the fatter the brush). Some paintbrushes may feel more comfortable than others. Buy good brushes that have even, thick bristles, and be sure to clean them thoroughly with soap and water after each use.

Other Painting Supplies You can use old saucers as palettes for acrylic and oil paints. For watercolors, keep a couple of cups on hand to hold the water. You will want to have some old clothes or an apron handy. Newspaper is useful for spreading out on your table surface or on the floor. You will also want to have some old rags and paper towels to clean up messes.

Miscellaneous Supplies Ruler, scissors, glue, stapler, scraps of fabric, old magazines, cardboard, and string are some of the things you will need to do the activities in this book.

Make your work space beautiful and decorate it with things that will inspire you.

followed him everywhere. It seemed to Leonardo that Francesco knew everything. As the boy and his uncle tramped through the vineyards and fields, Francesco taught Leonardo the names and uses of plants and herbs, the signs of approaching weather, and the habits of the wild animals who lived in the hills around Vinci. Francesco never tired of the curious boy's constant questions. "Tell me," Leonardo would say, "where the river begins." "Tell me what makes lightning." "Tell me what happens to the caterpillar inside its cocoon."

The local priest taught Leonardo how to read and write and how to use an abacus, but that was the only education Leonardo received. Instead, he spent many of his days wandering the countryside and studying nature. He explored the rocky crevasses of the hills around Vinci. He climbed along the banks of the river Arno and behind the crashing waterfalls. He walked through the fields of red poppies and blue cornflowers. He would jump on the bare back of one of his grandfather's horses and ride furiously down the dusty roads. Sometimes he would lay for hours beneath a tree, watching leaves move against the blue sky. He envied the birds as they soared over the hills and vineyards.

Sometimes he would turn his horse past the home of his mother. She had married since he was taken from her thatch and mud home. With her husband, Accattabriga the

As a child, Leonardo was always outdoors studying birds and plants. He found out that the best way to learn about something was to observe it carefully.

MATERIALS

Sketch pad or notebook
Pencil
Crayons or chalk
Tape recorder (optional)
Paper bag or small box

Take a walk to a nearby park or favorite place in nature and look for signs of animal life—birds' nests, anthills, cocoons, spiderwebs, animal tracks, and even dead bugs. Notice the different types of plants and trees and look closely at their bark, leaves, flowers, and seeds.

Observe the different colors, shapes, and textures all around you. When you find something that interests you, sit down with it a while and sketch it. Don't worry if you can't draw very well because this notebook is just for you.

Try making a bark rubbing by placing a piece of paper over the bark of a tree and rubbing over the paper with a crayon or chalk to pick up the pattern of the bark. Collect a leaf and seed from that tree. Do the same for other trees. Do the bark patterns differ? How many different shapes of leaves can you find?

Be as quiet as you can and listen attentively. Notice all the different sounds you hear. Do you hear birds, squirrels, planes, cars, running water, and your own breath? Use your tape recorder to record these sounds. Write down the time of day and all the sounds you hear in your notebook.

Collect interesting things you find like rocks, shells, leaves, flowers, and dead bugs. Place them in your bag or box. You might want to press your flowers under some heavy books and then glue them in your notebook. Later you will be able to study these things and use them in a still-life painting, collage, or other work of art as Leonardo did.

Quarreller, she raised crops on a few acres of land outside of town. She had another son and four daughters. She was always kind to Leonardo, but whenever he saw her, he felt sad and left out. She had her new family, and his own father was so far away and concerned with other things. Ser Piero's young wife, Albiera, died and he soon remarried another Florentine woman, Francesca. Leonardo barely knew this family of his.

Instead, Leonardo concerned himself with the world around him. He found everything interesting and everything he saw made him want to know more. He took paper and chalk with him on his walks to make sketches of all he saw. He studied the movements of birds and animals, the way the trees and plants grew, the rocks he found in the riverbeds, the light on the fields, and the shadows of the dense forests.

Leonardo's simple life in the country came to an end after his grandfather died and his Uncle Francesco married. His family decided he didn't belong in Vinci anymore and they agreed he should move in with his father and his new wife. The fourteen-year-old boy packed his few belongings and left the countryside for Florence.

Brush Up on Birds

When you draw or paint something, you notice things you may not have seen before. That's why Leonardo grew up to be a great artist and a great scientist. He was one of the first artists to draw things exactly as he saw them in nature. While sketching and painting birds, he learned a lot about their anatomy, or body structure.

MATERIALS

Watercolor paints
Paintbrush
Cup of water
Absorbent paper

Play with your paints! Get used to holding your brush and trying different strokes. See what it's like to use a little water or a lot on your brush. Mix paints to get new colors. Then, take your tools outside. Sit in your yard near a bird feeder or go to a park or the zoo—anyplace where you can find birds. Sit quietly until a bird lands nearby to model for you.

For the head, dab a wet brush into the paint. Hold the brush so it is vertical (straight up and down) to the paper. Press it down, then twist it to the right with your fingers. (These instructions are for right-handed artists. If you're left-handed, just reverse them.) To paint the bird's breast, dab some more paint on the brush and hold it horizontally (sideways) to the paper. Place it on the paper and pull it down toward you. For the wing, hold the brush vertically, press it down and draw it toward you. Taper off at the end by lifting up your hand. Paint the tail feathers by starting at the end of the tail. Hold the brush vertically and touch just the tip of it to the paper. Paint up toward the body. Fill in the details of the bird's legs, feet, and beak. Look for the distinctive markings and paint them in, using just a small amount of paint on the brush. Some birds have black eye masks, some have striped wings. Some birds have spotted breasts—hold the brush vertically and dot the paint onto the paper. To paint streaked markings, hold the brush the same way and make very small lines. You'll see that birds come in many different colors, shapes, and sizes.

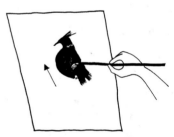

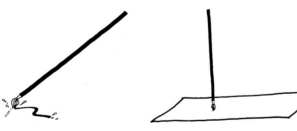

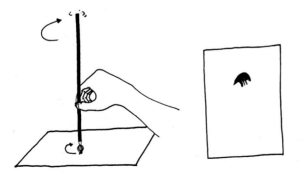

TWO

The Young Apprentice

T he great city of Florence! High walls topped by great towers circled the town. As he approached, Leonardo could see the roofs, towers, and steeples of Florence and the great dome of a cathedral. He couldn't wait to explore. As the guards at the city gate inspected his meager belongings, he fidgeted with excitement.

Florence was a trading center, a big and prosperous town, and people and goods from many different lands could be found there. Vendors hawked their wares in loud voices. Their tables were piled with beautifully dyed cloth, silks, and spices from faraway lands. Donkeys pulled heavy carts

Left: Detail from *Baptism of Christ*, **Andrea del Verrocchio and Leonardo da Vinci, 1472–75**

Right: Detail from *Adoration of the Magi*, **Leonardo da Vinci, 1481–82**

down the paved streets. Peasant folk shopped at stalls full of fruits and vegetables, meats and cheeses. The crowds parted as priests and great lords in velvet cloaks swept by. Leonardo gaped at all the people, the noise, and the confusion. He stared up at the large stone buildings of Florence, many topped with steep towers. He walked up the broad Via Larga on his way to his father's house, along with the donkeys and carts and throngs of people. The road took him past the famous Medici Palace and he wondered if he would ever see the powerful people who lived inside. The Medicis, a family of bankers and wealthy merchants, had ruled Florence for over one hundred years. Leonardo's new home was a great city, so different from his quiet village in the hills.

When he reached his father's home, he discovered he wasn't to remain there for long. Ser Piero decided it was time for the young man to learn a trade. At that time, it was normal for a boy of twelve or thirteen years to work. Girls worked at home until they were married, but families sent their sons to work as apprentices to merchants or craftsmen for a period of years.

What could Leonardo do? He had no real education, having been brought up in the country. His illegitimate birth prevented him from entering his father's profession as well as many others. Children whose parents were not married were not allowed to become doctors or lawyers or even to attend the university. Many guilds would not accept a young man of Leonardo's background.

But when Ser Piero looked at the drawings his son carried in his knapsack, he knew what Leonardo should do. He put the drawings in a fold of his sleeve and carried them to the "bottega" (which is the Italian word for studio or workshop) of the famous artist Andrea del Verrocchio.

Verrocchio was the greatest sculptor of the time and the official sculptor of the powerful Medici family. He had a square face, dark curly hair, and a serious expression that showed that work was his life. His eyes missed nothing, and as he looked at Leonardo's drawings he knew that this young man would come to be an artist even greater than he was. Verrocchio's bottega on Via de Agnolo was as busy as the streets of Florence. His workshop received orders for paintings, sculpture, household decorations, armor, jewelry, and many other items.

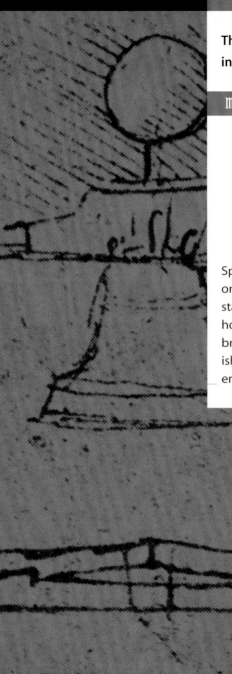

A Beaker for Brushes

This decorative jar for holding paintbrushes will look great in your bottega, or studio.

MATERIALS

Newspaper
Clear glass jar, empty and clean
Acrylic paints
Paintbrush

Spread newspaper out on your work surface. Hold the jar with one hand inside of it and paint a design on it. It's easiest to start at the bottom of the jar and work up. Let it dry for an hour. Use the jar to store brushes and pencils. (To help your brushes last longer, always clean them right after you've finished painting, then store them in your jar with the brush ends in the air.)

Leonardo's eyes opened wide when he saw Verrocchio's studio for the first time. The doors were open to the street and the teeming life of the city spilled inside. Playing children and their dogs ran through the rooms. Sometimes a pig or a chicken wandered in! Maestro Verrocchio stood in the middle of all the activity, alert to everything that was going on and directing the work of his young apprentices. Brushes and mallets and chisels hung on the walls, along with the sketches and plans of works in progress. One young man was firing up a kiln. Others hammered armor and pounded stone to powder. Easels, workbenches, and models stood everywhere.

Leonardo's father and Verrocchio shook hands. Young Leonardo was now apprenticed to the great artist. He would be a "discepolo" (which is the Italian word for an apprentice) and would spend many years learning to be an artist under the direction of Verrocchio.

Those years flew by. Leonardo grew up to be a handsome and strong young man. He worked long days and slept at night in the upstairs living quarters with the other apprentices. Maestro Verrocchio was kind but strict, and his apprentices worked very hard. For the first few months Leonardo did nothing but sweep the floor, clean paintbrushes, and listen to the talk of the other apprentices and

Portrait of a Musician, Leonardo da Vinci, 1490

Framed!

Pretend you're an apprentice in Verrocchio's bottega and make a picture frame. With these instructions you can make a frame for a small photograph of yourself or a friend.

MATERIALS

Scissors
Aluminum pie tin
Ruler
Pen (optional)
Piece of cardboard, 8 ½ by 11 inches
   (you can use the back of an empty cereal box)
Photograph, about 3 by 2 ½
White glue
Stapler

1

2

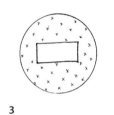

3

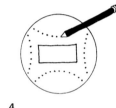

4

Cut out the bottom circle from an aluminum pie tin. (Be very careful not to hurt yourself on the sharp edges of the tin.) Cut a rectangle in the center of the circle measuring 3 by 2 ½ inches. This will be the front of your frame. Many pie tins have a design on them, but if yours doesn't, make a design on your frame by punching the tin from the back with a pen, being careful not to push the pen all the way through. Make a pattern all around the frame.

For the back, cut a piece of cardboard the same size as the front circle. Cut another piece of cardboard into a rectangle measuring 3 by 2½ inches. This will be the backrest for the frame. Center and glue your photograph onto the cardboard back. Place the tin front over the cardboard back, centering it over your photo. Staple the two pieces together along the edges of the circle. Glue ½ inch of the cardboard backrest to the back of the frame, about a third of the way from the bottom.

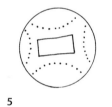

5

6

7

8

9

10

craftsmen. He watched everything that was going on. And in Verrocchio's bottega, there was so much going on! The wealthy people of Florence would come in to have their portraits painted. They asked Verrocchio to make items of silver and gold, armor and coats of arms, statues, dishes, and furniture. Verrocchio and his apprentices even made bells for churches and cannons used to guard the town. This work was done by the older apprentices.

Leonardo cleaned and swept. Eventually he was given the daily task of grinding pigments to make paint. After he mastered each task he was given a harder one. He polished bronze statues. He learned how to make paintbrushes. He prepared wooden panels for painting. He longed for the day when he would be able to use these materials and not just prepare them for another artist. In the meantime he sketched whenever he had time.

One day Verrocchio received a very important commission. Florence's cathedral, Santa Maria del Fiore, was nearly finished after almost two hundred years of construction. The final touch needed was a great bronze globe to be placed on the top. It would be a challenge to create, for the globe was to be twenty feet across and weigh over two tons. And not only would it be difficult to make—Verrocchio and his apprentices also had to figure out a way to install it on the top of the cathedral! Leonardo learned there was more to art than holding a paintbrush. The artists had to cast the globe in bronze, develop architectural plans, and even design the cranes and pulleys needed to install it. For this commission, art and engineering went hand in hand. In the workshop the apprentices calculated and designed for months. Plans covered the walls. On the spring day when it was installed, the whole town turned out to watch.

Meanwhile, there were still tombstones to create out of marble, death masks to make out of plaster, and coats of arms and banners to design. Leonardo was finally allowed to help on small assignments and he was happy to be using the brushes he had made. He painted the backgrounds of pictures. He also posed for a statue by Verrocchio. The Maestro captured Leonardo's fine features and thick, wavy hair in a figure of David.

The bottega was a favorite place for artists to gather and talk. Verrocchio's great talent attracted many artists who came to learn from him. Sometimes one of the apprentices would pick up a lute and sit in a corner and play. The young men argued about their ideas, teased each other about their progress, and taught each other new techniques.

Statue of David, Andrea del Verrocchio, 1476

People often asked Verrocchio to make death masks, masks of the faces of people who had died, as keepsakes of their loved ones. This is a life mask, one that displays your inner self—your interests, hobbies, and dreams.

MATERIALS

Scissors
Piece of cardboard, 8 1/2 by 11 inches (you can use the backing from a pad of paper)
Old magazines, postcards, and photographs
White glue
Crayons or colored markers
Paints (optional)
Paintbrush (optional)
Stapler
10-inch length of string

Cut out holes for the eyes, a nose, and a mouth from the cardboard. Cut out pictures, words, and phrases that represent the things you love from the magazines, postcards, and photographs. If you like sports, you might cut out pictures of people playing basketball. Do you have a pet? Maybe you will want to use a picture of your dog or cat. If you love nature, go out and collect leaves and flowers to include on your mask. Also, cut out words that describe you.

Make a collage of all of these pictures and words on the face of your mask, gluing them onto the cardboard. You can use crayons, markers, or paints to decorate the mask as well. Cover every part of the cardboard. Staple each end of the string to the back of the mask, about 3 inches from the top. Hang your mask on a wall.

We buy paint at the art supply store, but when Leonardo was an apprentice in Verrocchio's workshop he had to make his own. Oil paints were brought to Italy by visiting Flemish artists. Earlier artists used tempera paints and water-based paints. Painting with oil allowed artists to create different shades and to paint one layer over another without mixing up colors. The paint went on surfaces smoothly and didn't run.

Pigments (or colors) were made from many things, such as ground rocks, precious stones, and plants. Artists ground these into a fine powder and then mixed them with liquids like oil or water to make paint. The color ultramarine, a bright blue, was made from grinding up a precious stone called lapis lazuli. Artists made bright yellow by crushing crocuses. They even made brown paint using crushed mummies from Egypt! Black pigment came from burnt wood and soot, green from copper, and purple from crushed shellfish.

Before the introduction of oil paints, artists used tempera paint made by grinding the pigments into powder and mixing them with egg yolk. In Leonardo's time, they usually used this type of paint on wooden panels covered with linen. When painting murals with the "fresco" technique (see explanation on page 80), they used water-based paint. For a time, gold leaf was very popular. Artists would beat the gold into thin sheets and then press it on the surface of the painting.

Top: *The Tribute of Money,* Masacchio, 1427

Bottom: Detail of *Madonna Enthroned* (front of Maestra Altar), Duccio, 1308–11

14

Oil painting had just been introduced to Italy by visiting artists from northern Europe and Verrocchio's students were very excited about the new medium. Leonardo spent a lot of time mixing different materials to see what would make the best paint. He ground up different substances for pigments and mixed them with linseed or walnut oils. He tried new techniques to use with the oil paints. Leonardo had such great skill using the new medium that he soon surpassed all the others.

Another new idea the artists discussed was how to show perspective and depth in painting. Before Leonardo's time, objects and people in paintings were shown as flat and two-dimensional. The artists in Florence developed techniques to portray objects and people as having depth and as living in space. Leonardo learned to carefully calculate the placement of lines in his drawings and paintings to create this illusion of perspective. He used math and geometry to create his art.

It was an exciting time and the perfect place to be an artist. Florence was a great center for art and sculpture, and whenever Leonardo could leave the studio he went to look at these works of art. Leonardo spent many hours studying the frescoes and shrines and statues of Florence. He also sought out teachers in the fields of science, mathematics, and philosophy.

Kitchen Clay

In Verrocchio's studio, Leonardo learned how to make statues from bronze, marble, and terra-cotta. You can carve sculptures out of wax or soap, shape them from modeling clay from the store, or make this clay in your own kitchen.

MATERIALS

4 cups flour
1 cup salt
Bowl
1 1/2 cups water

Combine flour and salt in a bowl. Add water and mix together. Knead with your hands until it is smooth. If you'd like color, you can divide it up and add a couple of drops of food coloring to each piece, kneading until the color is incorporated. Your clay is now ready for molding into shapes, or it can be saved up to a week if you wrap it in plastic and store it in the refrigerator.

In paintings from the Middle Ages, objects and people looked flat and out of proportion. It was during the Renaissance that artists began to use perspective in their paintings and drawings. Artists began to draw things as they saw them in nature.

When you think about it, showing depth and space in a picture on a flat surface is no easy thing. Leonardo wrote about perspective in his notebooks. He said, "Among objects of equal size, that which is most remote from the eye will look the smallest." In the real world, the farther away things are, the smaller they look. Just look down a row of telephone poles and see for yourself. The poles closest to you look bigger than the ones farther away, even though they are the same size. In Renaissance art, like real life, the closer figures look larger and the farthest ones look smaller. You can see another example of perspective in the illustration of railroad tracks on page 27. The parallel lines seem to come together as they become more distant from you. In art, that point where the lines come together is called the vanishing point.

Perspective also refers to the way an object appears to change when you look at it from different points of view. If you look at a box straight on, you will see a square. If you look at it from another angle, you will see that it is a box, with depth and width.

Leonardo and his fellow artists used mathematics to plot the placement of objects in their paintings and drawings. They used other techniques to show perspective too, like shading and colors. They painted more distant objects and people in a blurry, unfinished way, which is what things look like when they're far away. The effect of greater distance was also created by using colors that were paler or with a blue tone.

Leonardo thought it was important for painters to understand how to use math and color to create a painting instead of just copying from other artists. He said that artists who painted without this knowledge were like sailors who get into a ship without a rudder or compass.

Top: Detail from *The Month of August* in *The Book of Hours*, The Limbourg Brothers, 1413–16

Bottom: *Christ Giving Keys to St. Peter*, Perugino, 1481

Detail from
*Madonna with
Child and Vase of
Flowers,* Leonardo
da Vinci, late
1470s

Leonardo lived in an exciting time during an era known to us as the Renaissance. The Renaissance began in Italy and spread to the rest of Europe, spanning the years from around 1400 to 1600.

The word Renaissance refers to the fascination people had at this time with ancient Greece and Rome. It is a French word meaning "rebirth" or "reawakening." People were rediscovering ideas about philosophy and art from these ancient times. They were also examining new ways of thinking and of expressing themselves.

Previous to this time, the Middle Ages (sometimes called the Dark Ages) stretched for many centuries. Pirates on the seas and robbers on land kept everyone frightened and close to their homes. People kept their heads down and questioned nothing. They lived their entire lives in the same village and were uninformed about events in the world.

Warfare was constant and brutal. Leaders rose from the villages and became lords of larger domains, with knights to serve them. As time went by only the great lords with large armies could hold their lands, and smaller kingdoms began to fall. Eventually nations formed. As the nations became larger and wealthier, systems of law became established, economies prospered, and the arts and sciences flourished.

Suddenly, people began to look beyond the superstitious and fearful world of the village. There was a renewed interest in the world and in mankind that became known as humanism. During the Renaissance there were great breakthroughs in anatomy, medicine, astronomy, and mathematics. The printing press was invented and books became available to people for the first time. It was also a time of world exploration and the beginning of modern science. Nicolaus Copernicus determined that the earth revolved around the sun. Many explorers sailed the seas in search of trade routes to the Far East. Christopher Columbus crossed the Atlantic to land in America. Vasco da Gama sailed around Africa and reached India. Magellan's voyagers circled the globe.

The artists of the Renaissance also explored new ways. Inspired by the spirit of the age, they experimented with many different techniques. They created the greatest art the world has ever known. Some of the early Renaissance artists Leonardo admired were Giotto and Masaccio. Many of the finest artists of Leonardo's time, such as Botticelli and Perugino, worked with him in Verrocchio's studio. Michelangelo lived at the Medici court. He created the magnificent sculpture of David and painted the ceiling of the Sistine Chapel in Rome. Other Renaissance painters include Titian and Raphael, whose creations are noted for their use of perspective and for their celebration of the individual and of nature.

With his questioning spirit and thirst for knowledge, Leonardo was entirely suited to this time. He explored so many new ideas in art and science that he is often referred to as a "Renaissance man."

Opposite page, top: Detail from *Expulsion of Adam and Eve,* Masaccio, 1425–28

Opposite page, bottom: Detail from *St. Michael Victorious,* Raphael, 1518

Top left: Detail from *Adoration of the Magi,* Botticelli, 1475

Top right: Detail from *Marriage of the Virgin,* Raphael, 1504

Bottom left: Detail from *Sacred and Profane Love,* Titian, 1514

Bottom right: Detail from *The Holy Family,* Michelangelo, 1503

Leonardo began to think that everything was connected in some way, and he wanted to learn it all. He used what he learned in his paintings and drawings. And just like he did as a child, he took paper and chalk with him everywhere and sketched everything he saw.

Some of the things that Leonardo liked to sketch most were animals. He studied birds' wings so he could paint the wings of angels in a realistic way. Leonardo loved horses and spent hours at stables watching the way they moved and sketching them.

Leonardo felt strongly that an artist must learn from nature and draw inspiration from what he or she observes. He thought it was important to thoroughly understand a thing in order to paint it.

This passion for observation began to show in Leonardo's work. The plants and flowers in his paintings looked exactly as they did in the fields. His portraits were so realistic, it was as if the people were right there. Eventually he graduated from his apprenticeship and became a "garzone," or journeyman.

His father stopped by the bottega one day and asked Leonardo for a favor. "Would you paint something on the front of a shield for a friend of mine?" he asked. Leonardo took the wooden shield and smoothed it down and prepared its surface. He thought carefully about the use of a shield while trying to decide what to paint on it. A shield held

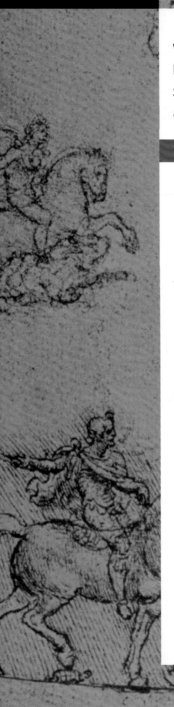

When Leonardo was a young apprentice in Florence, he spent all of his spare time drawing. Often, he went to the Medici family's private zoo and drew the animals there. Take a trip to the zoo to sketch the animals or draw your pet at home.

MATERIALS

Pencils (see page 2 for recommendations)
Sketch pad

The most important thing to do when learning how to draw is to learn how to look. Study Leonardo's sketches of horses. What is special about the shape? The parts of the body? Note the horse's rounded haunches, barrel-shaped body, and powerful muscles. These are the features you will want to emphasize. The second most important thing to do is practice. Even if you think you can't draw, give it a try. Can you draw circles and ovals? That's all you need to start.

Draw the animal using geometric shapes. For the horse, you might start by lightly drawing a large circle for his rear, a long oval for his body, and another circle for his chest. Draw his neck and head as ovals. Draw narrow cylinders for his legs and small ovals for his feet. While making this preliminary sketch, notice proportion (for instance, the size of the head compared to the body). Go over the shapes, building on them with heavier lines. Hold and move the pencil in different ways to get different effects. Draw soft, shaded lines lightly with the side of the pencil. Press down hard and move it back and forth for a hard, jagged line. Pencil in the distinctive features, such as the hooves and tail. For the horse, use soft, short strokes with the pencil held slightly at an angle to capture the texture of his hair. Use longer lines of different sizes for his flowing mane.

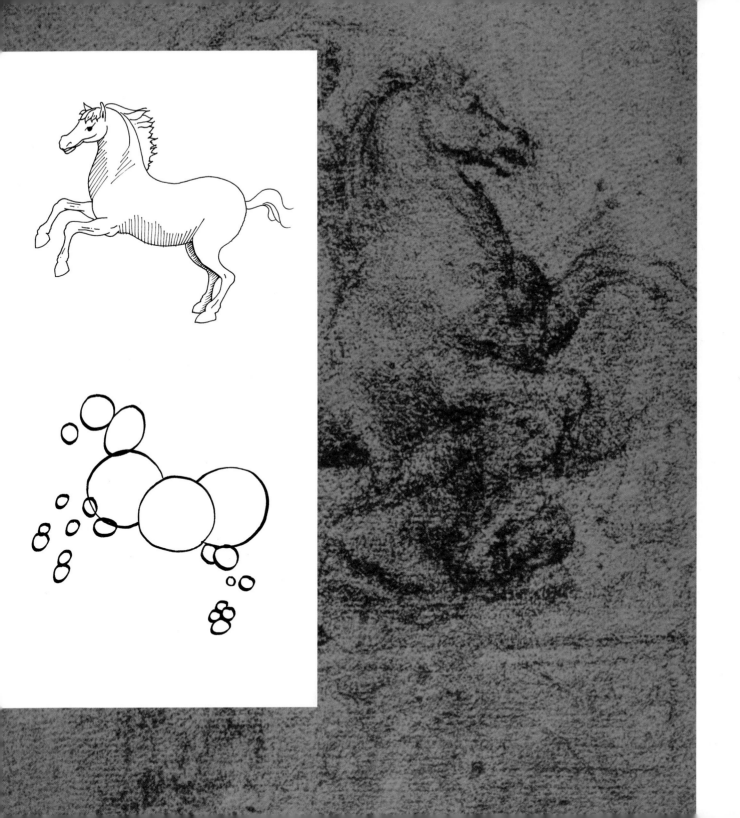

Make yourself a master of perspective, then acquire perfect knowledge of the proportions of men and other animals.

—Leonardo

Detail from
Baptism of Christ,
Andrea del
Verrocchio and
Leonardo da Vinci,
1472–75

up to an enemy in battle should present a terrifying image, he thought. He decided to decorate it with a painting of a menacing dragon.

Whenever he could get away, Leonardo wandered out to the countryside and came back to his room with his pockets full of the strangest things. He collected lizards and beetles, the skeletons of birds, scorpions and toads, bats and snakes. He used parts of all of these creatures as models to draw a monstrous dragon, a frightening mix of horns and tail, teeth and wings. He painted the dragon coming out of a cave with fierce eyes and fire flaring from its nostrils. When he finished he placed the shield on an easel and pulled a curtain over the window so that only a shaft of sunlight fell on it. Then he called on his father to tell him the shield was finished.

When Ser Piero walked into the dark room his eyes fell on the sun-lit dragon. He stood frozen with fear. Leonardo knew then that his work was good. The shield would stop any enemy in his tracks.

Maestro Verrocchio put Leonardo to work on part of a painting that he was working on, *Baptism of Christ.* He had Leonardo paint one of the angels in this work. When Verrocchio saw the angel that Leonardo painted, he was stunned. It was so beautiful and so much better than his own work that Verrocchio vowed he would never touch a paintbrush again.

In 1472, when Leonardo was twenty years old, he became a master craftsman of his trade. He had earned the right to the title of Maestro. He stayed at Verrocchio's bottega and worked with him for a few more years. He started to receive a few commissions of his own. He painted *The Annunciation*, a beautiful painting of the angel Gabriel appearing to Mary. He took special care to paint the wings of the angel so that they resembled the birds he studied so carefully. He painted a portrait of a Florentine lady, Ginevra, encircling her head with a halo of juniper. This was a visual play on words.

Ginevra's name was similar to the Italian word for the juniper bush, "ginepro."

But life wasn't all work. There was plenty of opportunity for fun in Florence, where nearly every month there was a carnival, tournament, or parade. Leonardo enjoyed parties and liked to wear fine clothes. He loved to ride horses and play music. He wrote poems and riddles and jokes.

Lorenzo de Medici was the powerful head of the ruling family of Florence. He was young and handsome and he liked hunting, dancing, and poetry. He was known throughout Florence as Lorenzo the Magnificent.

The Annunciation,
Leonardo da Vinci,
1473–75

23

Lorenzo often held great parties and tournaments and always hired Verrocchio and his apprentices to create wonderful backdrops and floats for these events. They also made carnival masks and disguises for people attending the parties.

On the days when carnivals were held, all of Florence left work to celebrate. From every window tapestries and garlands of flowers hung down the stone walls. All of the church bells rang. Friars sang ballads in the streets. Banners in the city's colors of red and white flew in the wind. Everyone dressed in their finest clothes and stood on their balconies and roofs to watch the event. Falconers with hawks on their wrists and dog keepers, each with ten panting dogs to a leash, paraded by. Fine lords and ladies in carriages waved. Trumpets blared and horses and riders filed by, led by pages carrying banners. These were the competitors for the tournaments, the "jousters," on their fine horses. The jousting went on all day in the Piazza Santa Croce. Leonardo watched it all with great excitement. At the end of the day Lorenzo would lead dancers through the streets.

The townspeople loved the tournaments, but they didn't all love the Medici family. Another great family of Florence, the Pazzi family, plotted against Lorenzo. One day Lorenzo and his brother Giuliano attended mass at the cathedral. As the bell rang for the end of the service, the Pazzi conspirators entered the church with swords in their hands and attacked the Medici brothers. Giuliano was killed immediately, but Lorenzo drew his sword and kept the killers at bay until people heard his cries and came to help.

Leonardo was asked to create an altarpiece for a monastery. The monks chose the subject of the painting, and Leonardo drew many preliminary sketches for *the Adoration of the Magi*. In this painting, the three "Magi," or wise men, come bearing gifts to the Christ child. Other men and animals stand looking on in wonder. Leonardo experimented with various compositions. He calculated lines of perspective. Though he worked on this painting for a very long time, he never finished it. It was perhaps the first, but not the last, time that Leonardo would leave a work unfinished. Although unfinished, the painting showed Leonardo's great talent. He placed the main figures in the painting—Mary, the Christ child, and the three magi—in a pyramid, which gave balance to the work. Also, while most of the artists of his time showed their subjects clearly outlined, Leonardo painted his subjects by using a subtle combination of light and shadow. The people in his paintings seemed to emerge from the shadows into the light. This technique of Leonardo's, the use of light and dark, is known as "chiaroscuro."

Great families, knights, and guilds (associations of merchants or craftsmen) all had banners, each with colors and patterns of special significance. Many showed animals symbolizing qualities such as strength (a bear) and courage and generosity (a lion). The Medici emblem showed six pills (historians think that's because someone in the family was a doctor). Create a special banner for your family.

chevron   cross   fess

MATERIALS

Pencil
Several sheets of drawing paper, 8½ by 11 inches
Ruler
Scissors
Felt fabric in your favorite color, about 3 by 2½ feet
Assorted smaller pieces of felt in a variety of colors
Needle
Thread
Dowel rod, ⅜ inch in diameter and 36 inches long
Assorted buttons, ribbons, beads, or sequins (optional)
Piece of string, about 48 inches long

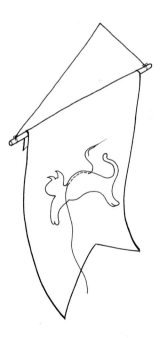

With your pencil, draw your designs on paper. You could use a pattern from the Middle Ages, such as an upside-down "v" called a "chevron," a cross, or a "fess," which is a wide band running across the middle. Animal symbols were often used on shields and banners during the Middle Ages. You might think of other images that are good symbols for your family. Do you all have big feet? Make a giant shoe! A design for an artistic family might include a palette with 4 or 5 circles of paint on it.

After you have drawn your designs on paper, cut them out to use as stencils. Fold the large felt piece down 1 inch at the top (the top should be about 2½ feet wide). Use your needle and thread to baste, or sew, this flap down all the way across the top to create a tunnel to run the dowel rod through. At the bottom, cut a triangle so that your banner will have two tails. Place the stencils over the smaller felt pieces and cut out your designs. Sew them on the banner. You can also sew on decorative buttons, ribbons, beads, or sequins if you like. Slide the dowel rod into the top of the banner. Tie the string to each end of the dowel rod and hang your banner up on a wall.

*Adoration of the
Magi,* **Leonardo da
Vinci, 1481–82**

Leonardo was still learning and his work was excellent, but he began to feel discouraged. He was having problems getting paid by the monks. Other young artists were advancing and getting better commissions. He felt unappreciated in Florence and began to wonder if he could ever make his own way there. He had been happy during his stay with Verrocchio, but now he felt confined. He wanted to stretch his wings.

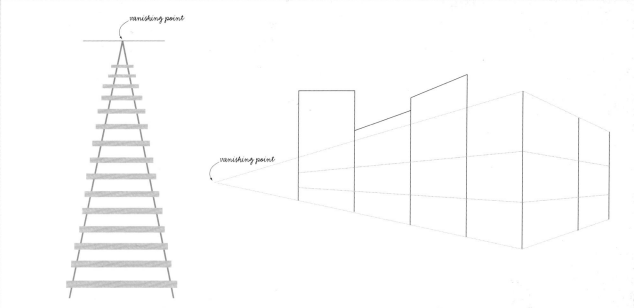

Look at the drawing of the railroad tracks. It's easy to find the vanishing point in this picture. It's the spot where the parallel lines of the tracks appear to come together in the distance.

Now look at this drawing of buildings. Does something look odd? Out of place? You can probably tell that the building on the left is drawn incorrectly. It is out of perspective. If you drew an imaginary line along the tops and bottoms of the buildings into the distance, those lines would all come together at one place—the vanishing point. However, the line drawn from the top of the left building would not.

See if you can find the vanishing point in other drawings. Look at the illustration of *The Last Supper* (see page 56). If you draw imaginary lines along the tops of the doors toward the middle of the painting, they will meet at the top of Jesus' head. Lines that follow the angle of the ceiling do the same. Leonardo designed this painting so that the vanishing point would be directly at the head of Jesus. The viewer's eyes are automatically drawn to the vanishing point.

Right: Drawing for a city on two levels, Leonardo da Vinci, early 1490s

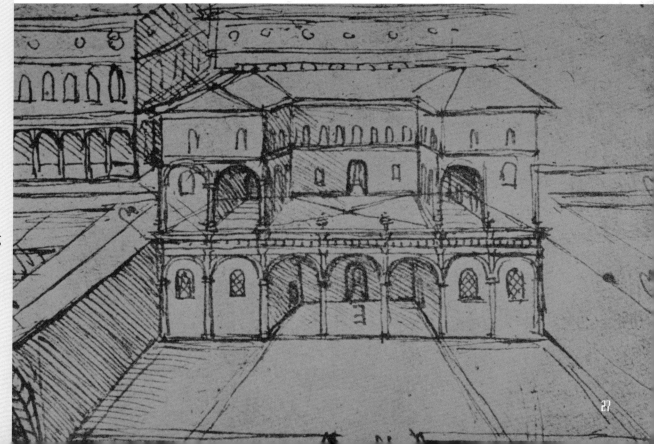

Detail from
The Benois Madonna,
Leonardo da Vinci,
1480

THREE

A Genius at Work

Leonardo had seen the ruler of Milan, Ludovico Sforza, during one of the festivals in Florence. Ludovico was a powerful and ambitious man. He was large, with dark hair, dark skin, and black eyes. He acted as regent for his young nephew, Gian, who was supposed to rule Milan one day. But everyone knew that Ludovico would never give up his reign. Whatever his ambitions, it was said that Ludovico was a great patron of artists. Leonardo heard, too, that Milan was an exciting place, a city where scholars, doctors, scientists, and mathematicians gathered. He wanted very much to go to Milan and decided that he would offer his services to this man, Ludovico.

So, at the age of thirty, Leonardo left Florence for Milan, bearing a gift and a letter for Ludovico. He made his way to the city and through its narrow streets to the Castello Sforzesco, a formidable fortress. He walked across the drawbridge under the eyes of the archers on the guard towers. Once inside, he was escorted through a long yard and into an inner fortress. All of the guards made him nervous, but the sight of the gardens and courtyards and people in beautiful dress soon made him feel more at ease.

Right: Diagram of human proportions, Leonardo da Vinci, 1492

The gift Leonardo brought was a "lira da braccio," a type of stringed instrument called a lute, that he had made of silver. It was a beautiful instrument made in the shape of a horse's head. He stood before Ludovico dressed in a rose-colored tunic, with his long curly beard reaching down to the middle of his chest. He lifted the lute and played. Leonardo had taught himself to play music and his talent astonished Ludovico and his court. He then

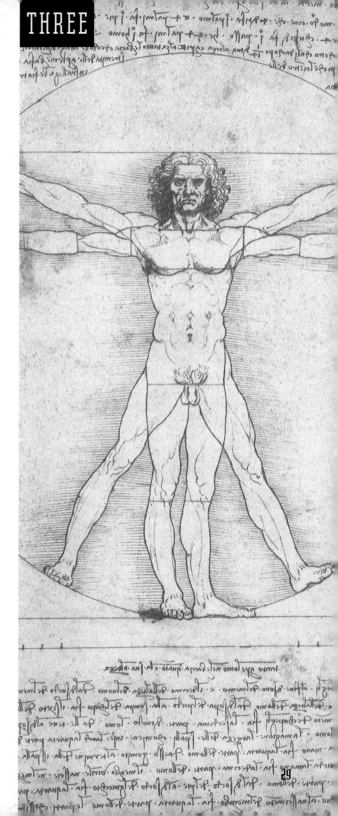

Leonardo offered himself as a military engineer to Ludovico, listing the following services he felt he could provide:

I can make bridges extremely light and strong and easily carried. With them you may pursue and flee from the enemy. Also, I have methods of burning and destroying those of the enemy.

If you are besieging a fortress, I know how to take the water out of the moats and can make bridges and ladders to scale walls.

I have methods for destroying every kind of fortress.

I have machines that can fling small stones until they almost resemble a storm. With the smoke of these I can cause great terror to the enemy, to his great detriment and confusion.

If the fight should be at sea, I have many machines most efficient for offense and defense and vessels that will resist the attack of the largest guns and powder.

I have ways to make tunnels without noise in order to reach a designated spot, even if it is under a trench or a river.

I can make covered chariots, safe and unattackable. When they enter among the enemy with their artillery no one can break them.

If needed I can make big guns of fine and useful forms.

I can contrive catapults and other marvelous machines not in common use.

In times of peace I can give perfect satisfaction to the equal of any other in architecture and the composition of buildings public and private, and in guiding water from one place to another.

I can carry out sculpture in marble, bronze, or clay and also in painting whatever may be done, as well as any other. Furthermore, a bronze horse could be made to glorify and honor the lord your father of blessed memory of the illustrious house of Sforza.

If any of the above named things seem to anyone to be impossible, I am most ready to make the experiment whenever you please.

I commend myself with the utmost humility to Your Excellency.

Ludovico hired him immediately and Leonardo worked for him for seventeen years.

Angel with Lute, Associate of Leonardo da Vinci, 1490s

offered the lute to Ludovico along with the letter. The letter outlined for Ludovico the services Leonardo could provide for him. Leonardo told him he could design weapons and fortifications that would keep his city safe from any enemy. Ludovico was pleased. "Eccellente," he said. "I have many enemies."

Leonardo had studied in an artist's workshop for many years—yet he was now presenting himself as a military engineer! This was not as strange as it may seem. Leonardo was fascinated by technology and curious about the workings of machines. He studied and sketched them as much as he did birds and plants. He had learned the art of casting metal and designing armor from Verrocchio. In his spare time he invented machines and weapons such as fire throwers and missiles. He even made an early design for a machine gun. His inventions were not like anything anyone had ever seen before.

Milan became Leonardo's new home. One of the greatest cities of Europe, it lay in a plain surrounded by rivers. To the north and west rose the great mountains of the Alps and beyond them was France. Dirty canals ran through the town and old, Gothic buildings towered overhead. The streets were narrow mazes, crowded

Leonardo's silver lute captured the heart of Ludovico. You can make a musical instrument from items found around the house. Adult supervision is recommended for this activity.

MATERIALS

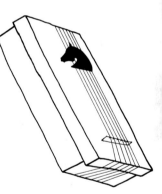

Pencil
Empty shoe box with lid
Utility knife
Piece of cardboard, about 1½ by 3 inches
Scissors
Ruler
Tape
Newspapers
Silver spray paint
6 rubber bands of varying thickness

Draw a horse's head (approximately 3 by 3 inches) at one end of the lid of the shoe box. Ask an adult to help you cut the shape out carefully with a utility knife. Make a 1½ inch slit in the lid of the box 3 inches from the other end as shown. Make a bridge for the lute out of the small square of cardboard. Cut it into a T-shape so that the bottom of the bridge is 1½ inches and the top is 3 inches. Make 6 slits in the top of the bridge. Insert the bridge into the slit in the box. (The bridge will raise the "strings" off the box, making the sound better.) Tape the lid firmly to the bottom of the box.

Now take the project outside or to a well-ventilated area. Spread the newspaper out and spray paint the box and bridge with the silver paint. Leave it several hours to dry. When dry, stretch the rubber bands around the box, putting each one through one of the slits in the bridge.

Leonardo was left-handed and wrote backwards. No one is sure why, but it certainly stopped people from reading over his shoulder! Use this backwards alphabet to learn to write like Leonardo.

All you need is a piece of plain paper and a pen. Here is the alphabet as it would be seen in a mirror:

ƧYXWVUTƧЯϘꟼ0ИMⴃ᚛ꞀИꓶⵁᖷꟼƎꓒꓛꓭA

Write a message in mirror writing and send it to your friends. They'll have to hold the paper up to a mirror to read your secret message.

Study of the hand and arm,
Leonardo da Vinci, 1510

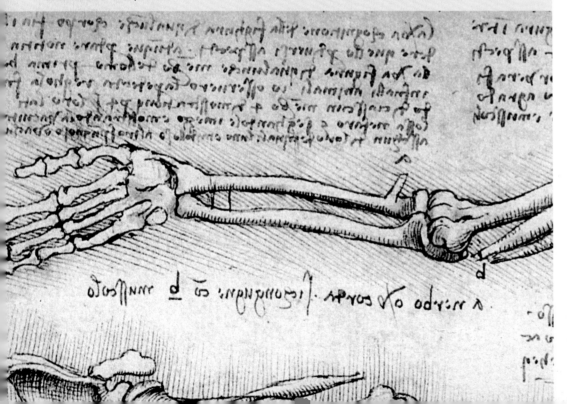

with the shops of goldsmiths, tapestry weavers, armorers, and silk merchants.

Leonardo found a place to live with the Predis brothers, who were artists. He soon made himself at home in Milan. He made friends with other artists and musicians and visited the university to listen to lectures and talk with scholars. Books were scarce at that time, so Leonardo sought them out and borrowed them whenever he could.

Wherever he went he carried a small sketchbook slung from his belt. He wrote constantly, jotting down his observations of nature and writing his thoughts. He drew pictures of people he saw in the streets and made sketches of inventions. He wrote his ideas and descriptions in reverse script, so that they could only be read if held up to a mirror. He wrote everything down as it came to him, thinking someday he would rewrite his notes and organize them into books.

In the middle of a description of a land-scape Leonardo would jot down a note about a book he wanted to read: "Get Messer Fazio to show you the book on proportion." On a page about geometry and river canals he wrote what he'd eaten for lunch that day: "frutta, minestrone, insalata" (fruit, minestrone soup, salad).

In a way, these notes are a reflection of how Leonardo's mind worked. Everything he did reminded him of something else. He liked to draw patterns of intertwined curves

Leonardo was never without a notebook which he carried slung from his belt. Here's how you can make one. Adult supervision is recommended for this activity.

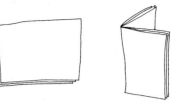

MATERIALS

10 sheets of drawing paper, 9 by 12 inches

Darning needle

Thread

Thimble

Scissors

2 pieces of cardboard, 7 by 10 inches each, (backs from pads of paper work well)

1 piece of cardboard, 1/2 inch wide by 10 inches long

Ruler

White glue

Sturdy fabric, in your favorite color and design, about 1/2 yard

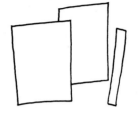

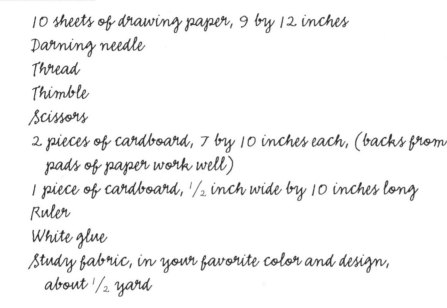

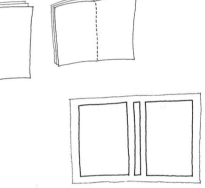

Baste, or sew, the paper together in the middle using your needle, thread, and thimble. Tighten the thread and tie it at each end with a knot. Use your 2 pieces of equal size cardboard for the covers of your notebook and the 1/2 inch by 10 inch piece for the spine of your notebook. Lay the fabric out smoothly and glue the three pieces of cardboard onto the fabric. Leave a little gap between each piece of cardboard so the notebook will be easy to open and close. Cut the fabric, leaving a 1/2 inch of extra material along the edges. Fold the fabric over the cardboard and glue it down. Open the paper in the middle and place it on top of the cardboard covers. Glue the bottom piece of paper to the cardboard cover on each side.

   Use your notebook as Leonardo did: as a journal to write down your thoughts (in mirror writing, of course), as a sketchbook to draw people or trees and plants on nature walks, and as a notebook of inventions and ideas.

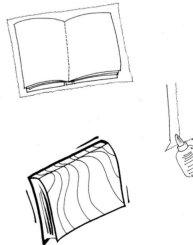

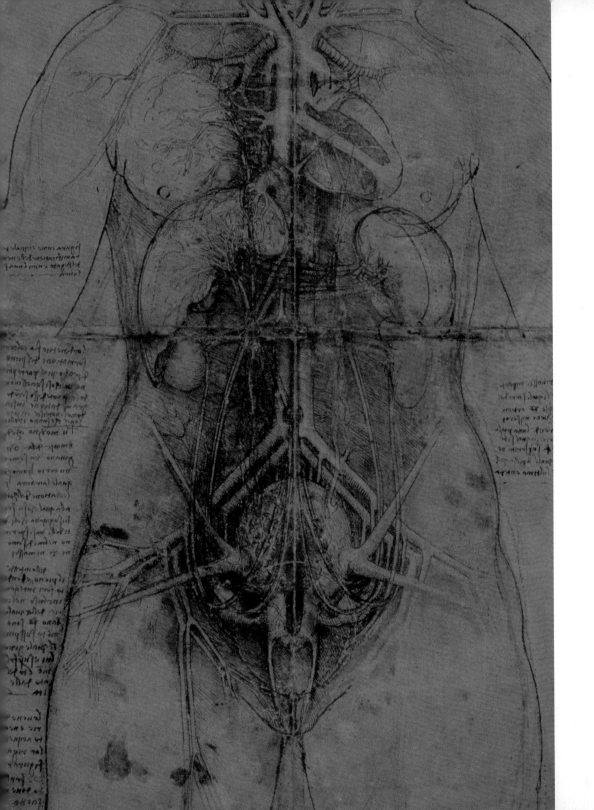

Anatomical study of a woman's body, Leonardo da Vinci, 1506–08

and knots. They seemed to symbolize his belief that all things are connected.

His friendships with musicians led him to study the science of sound and he illustrated a work on harmony. When some ancient Roman ruins were discovered, it sparked his interest in architecture. He drew a plan for a dome for the cathedral of Milan. He saw a total eclipse and invented a device to look at the sun without harming his eyes. Leonardo wrote in his notebook, "il sole non si muove" (the sun does not move). This was a remarkable observation. In Leonardo's day people thought the sun revolved around the earth.

He also became interested in anatomy. Leonardo's passion for painting first led him to an interest in the human body and the more he learned the more he wanted to know. He went to hospitals to watch doctors operate on people. He visited morgues alone at night to dissect

All our knowledge has its origin in our perceptions.

—Leonardo

As he measured and drew human bodies, Leonardo noticed that we generally have standard proportions. He noted that "the span of a man's outstretched arms is equal to his height." Other observations he noted about human proportions:

• In an adult, the head is one-eighth of the person's height.

• The face is divided into three equal parts—from the chin to the nostrils, from the nostrils to the eyebrows, and from the eyebrows to the hairline.

• The distance across the face from one ear to another is the same as that from the eyebrows to the chin.

• The ear is as long as the nose.

• The length of the forearm up to the elbow is one fourth of the body's height.

• The foot is one-half as long as the distance from the heel to the knee.

• The distance from elbow to wrist is one-half the length of the thighbone.

Now is your chance to test Leonardo's observations and maybe make some of your own.

MATERIALS

Newspaper
Tape
Black marker
Measuring tape

Spread several sheets of newspaper on the floor so that it is longer and wider than you are. Tape them together. Lay down on the paper with your arms held out away from your body and have a friend draw the outline of your body with a black marker on the paper. Measure the different parts of your body and see if they fit into the general proportions that Leonardo noted. Have your friend measure the parts of your face to see if those proportions Leonardo noted are true.

the bodies of those who had died. He measured muscles and described their functions in his notes. He drew intricate diagrams of the organs. He discovered the way blood flows throughout the body and made important discoveries about lungs and oxygen. Eventually he came to know more about anatomy than the doctors of his time. Leonardo's anatomical sketches were the first such detailed scientific drawings of the human body.

He began to apply many of his theories about anatomy to his work in art and science. With his new knowledge of the human body, he was able to paint people more realistically. He even designed buildings with the human body in mind. All of his interests seemed to converge.

Even though he had all of these new pursuits, Leonardo continued to paint. He proved to his new patron, Ludovico, that he had many talents. Ludovico had him paint a portrait of his lady friend, Cecilia Gallerani. He called this painting *Lady with Ermine*. A poet said about this painting that it was so lifelike that "Nature herself was jealous."

Lady with Ermine,
Leonardo da Vinci,
1485

Opposite: *Virgin of the Rocks,*
Leonardo da Vinci,
1483–86

He also got a commission, along with two of the Predis brothers, to create an altarpiece. For this he painted *Virgin of the Rocks*.

> *A painter above all must keep his mind as clear as the surface of a mirror.*
>
> —Leonardo

His painting of Mary with the infants Jesus and John the Baptist and a beautiful angel was striking and unusual. The placement of the figures in the painting created a sense of unity and peace, and the realism of the rocks and plants was astonishing. Leonardo used an effect in this painting known as "sfumato," or smoke. In his landscapes, objects in the distance seemed to vanish like smoke, just like in real life. It was a way to show distance and perspective. His use of the technique of chiaroscuro (painting figures by contrasting light and shadow) was perfected, and the tones and colors of the painting showed he had mastered paint and brush like no one ever before.

In 1484 the plague struck Milan. For several years, thousands of people suffered and died from the horrible disease. The healthy, including Ludovico and his court, abandoned Milan for the country, while the sick died and were left to rot in the streets. Leonardo

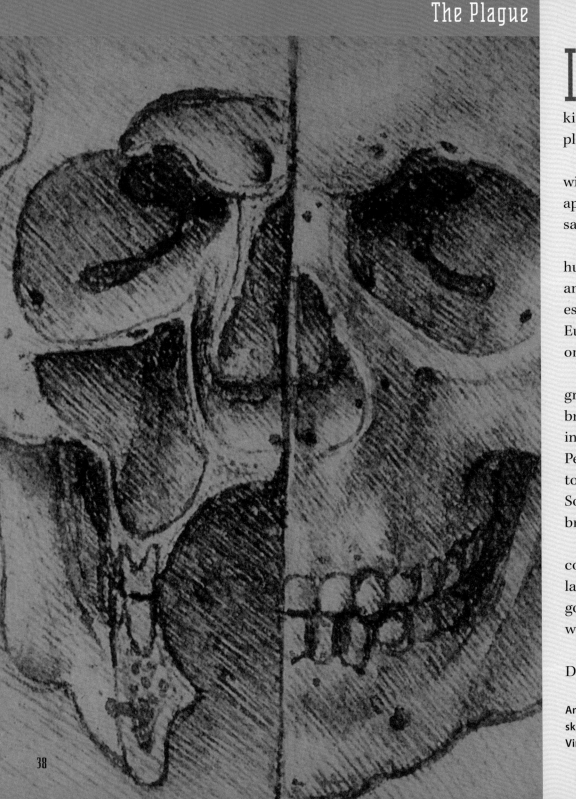

Italy and the rest of Europe suffered from terrible epidemics a number of times during the Middle Ages and the Renaissance. There were several kinds of plagues, but the worst was the bubonic plague, also known as The Black Death (1348–1350).

Explorers and traders brought the illness back with them from their voyages. The Black Death first appeared in Europe in 1347, when a ship of Genoese sailors returned from Asia. The entire crew was sick.

The illness quickly swept across Europe and hundreds of thousands of people died. Whole cities and regions were wiped out by the epidemic. It is estimated that 25 to 45 percent of the population of Europe died from the highly contagious disease and one-third of the population of Italy died.

The sickness started with large swellings in the groin and armpit areas after which blotches and bruises appeared on the body. Generally, once infected with the plague, the victim died within days. People did not know how the illness spread or how to prevent it. Some thought it was the wrath of God. Some thought they could protect themselves by breathing through herbs.

Conditions were worse in the cities than in the countryside. Rich people left the cities to stay in isolated villas in the country. The poor, with nowhere to go, suffered the most. Bodies piled up in the streets while grave diggers tried to keep up with the work.

The plague returned many times after The Black Death and several times during Leonardo's lifetime.

Anatomical study of
skull, Leonardo da
Vinci, 1489

even found subject for thought in this horrible epidemic and turned his attention to disease prevention. He thought the narrow and dirty streets and poor sanitation of the town had spread the disease. So he designed a layout for the city that featured wide streets and canals and proper sewage disposal. He designed a system for washing the streets automatically with a system of special locks and paddle wheels. Leonardo's town design was two-tiered, with the bottom streets used for deliveries and wagons, and the top streets for homes and churches. When the plague of the 1480s ended the whole city was ready to celebrate. Ludovico hired architects and artists and builders to create new buildings and gardens, to widen and pave the streets, and to create fountains and statues and works of art. Leonardo became a common sight at the Sforza castle. Eventually he became Ludovico's top artist

Drawing for a city on two levels, Leonardo da Vinci, early 1490s

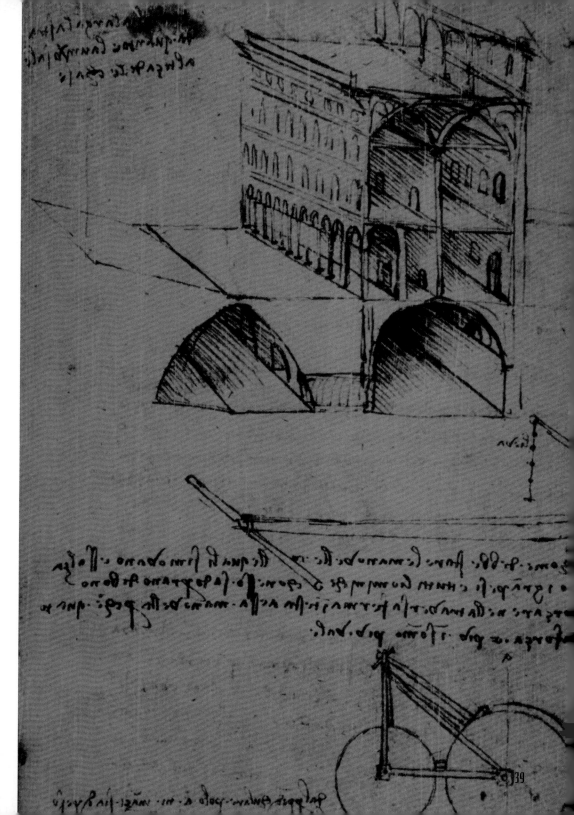

When fortune comes seize her firmly by the forelock, for, I tell you, she is bald at the back.

—Leonardo

and engineer, or "pictor et ingeniarius ducalis" as he was called in Latin.

In 1489 Ludovico arranged his nephew's marriage to Isabella of Aragon. He asked Leonardo to create a marriage pageant for the bride and groom. Leonardo's Feast of Paradise and Masque of the Planets had people talking for months. There was dancing and a masked procession into the great hall of the castle. Paintings all around the hall showed episodes from history and the great deeds of the Sforza family. At midnight the music stopped and a curtain went up. In front of the hushed crowd was the inside of a huge hemisphere. Stars and planets and the twelve signs of the zodiac made out of torch-lit glass rotated in their orbits, moved by hidden mechanisms. Actors dressed in elaborate costumes symbolizing the planets each presented a special wish in verse to the couple on the occasion of their marriage. Ludovico was so pleased that he had Leonardo create another pageant when he married his wife, Beatrice. Every month there was another cause for celebration to keep Leonardo occupied.

Finally, Leonardo had his own bottega. He was so busy that he needed assistance, so he took on five apprentices of his own. His studio was always crowded with people. Artists came there to talk and admire his work. Musicians played and sang. Scholars read poetry. Everyone wanted to be his

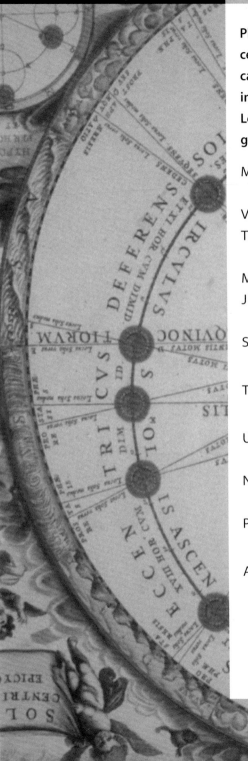

A Masque of the Planets

Plan a Masque of the Planets for your next birthday party or to celebrate Leonardo's birthday, April 15th. Each of your friends can choose a planet to personify. Make up costumes representing your planet and write a poem for the occasion, just like Leonardo did. The planets are named after ancient Roman gods, each with his or her own personality and traits.

MERCURY—the messenger is often portrayed wearing a helmet with wings at his feet.

VENUS—named for the goddess of love and beauty.

TELLUS—our own planet Earth is also called Gaea, or mother.

MARS—this reddish planet is named after the god of war.

JUPITER—named for the ruler of the gods, who is often portrayed hurling bolts of lightning from the sky.

SATURN—the planet with rings around it was named after Jupiter's father, an ancient god.

These were all the planets Leonardo knew about. After his time, three more planets were discovered.

URANUS—a name for heaven. Uranus was the first father (as Tellus was the first mother).

NEPTUNE—named after the god of the sea, who always carried a three-pronged fork.

PLUTO—a very small planet named for the lord of the underworld.

A poem by Mercury might go something like this:

> I come today on winged feet
> To bring you this special birthday treat,
> And messages from far and near
> Wishing you a happy day and year!

friend. It was said that "one only had to see him for all sadness to vanish." Leonardo would arrange feasts for his friends and spend whole evenings telling them outrageous jokes and stories to make them laugh. Or he would perform tricks, like making multicolored flames with special chemicals or breaking a piece of wood balanced on two glasses without cracking them. Leonardo was also very strong, and his friends often dared him to show his strength by bending a horseshoe with his bare hands. He observed their faces and gestures carefully as they laughed at his jokes and tricks, and after they left he drew their expressions so perfectly that everyone who saw the drawings laughed as hard as those who had been at the feast.

All along Leonardo continued to create new inventions. He designed a hot air-powered spit and a water-powered alarm clock. A machine to move monuments and musical instruments including a carillon and a recorder were also among his inventions. He developed new theories about optics and vision that brought him to the conclusion that light traveled in waves. In his studies of the nature of light and sound, he was the first to liken their motion to the motion of waves. He made discoveries about the anatomy of the eye, figuring out the problem of farsightedness and the principle of stereoscopic vision. He designed a type of contact

Leonardo enjoyed telling stories and jokes and liked to make people laugh. He often told his scary "prophecies," common occurrences described in such a way that they seemed horrible and frightening. They are what we call riddles. Can you figure them out?

1. Men will walk and not move, talk to those who are not present, and hear those who do not speak.

2. Likenesses of men and animals will follow them wherever they go.

3. The waters of the sea will rise above the mountains and fall on the homes of men.

4. Out of cavernous pits shall come forth that which will make all the nations of the world toil and sweat with great torment, anxiety and labor, that they may gain its aid.

5. One shall arise from small beginnings that will rapidly become great. It shall have respect for no created thing, but by its power it shall transform almost everything from its natural condition into another.

Answers: 1. Dreaming 2. Shadows 3. Evaporation of water into clouds, then rain 4. Gold 5. Fire

lens. A telescope was also invented by Leonardo. In his notes he wrote ideas about water fountains, watches, a machine to press olives, an automatic door closer, folding furniture, table lamps, and locks for chests.

Soon Leonardo had another project to occupy his mind. Ludovico wanted a monument created to honor his father—a large statue of a bronze horse and rider to display as proof of his family's power. He wanted it to be huge! Grandissimo! All the artists of Milan hoped for the honor of creating this monument and there was a great competition. Of course Ludovico gave the commission to Leonardo.

It was a challenging assignment. No one knew how to cast such a large bronze piece. Leonardo studied and sketched and designed. He would disappear for hours, only to be found in the stables sketching the horses, noting their weight, their muscles, and their movements. While he was there, he designed a model stable with gutters and automatic feeders and pumps to fill the troughs! If he couldn't be found in the stables or on the streets looking at statues, then his apprentices could find him in the foundries making notes on recipes for alloys and studying the techniques of casting bronze. Leonardo made molds and tested many different materials to use for his statue. He even designed special furnaces.

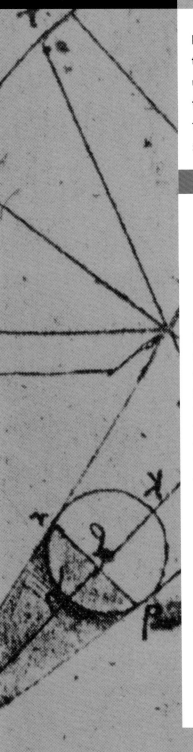

Eye Exercises

Being a painter made Leonardo very curious about the function of the eye. He discovered that having two eyes working together allows us to judge distance and depth. Each one of our eyes sees an object from a slightly different viewpoint. An image travels from each eye to our brain, which uses the combined images to calculate the exact shape and placement of the object we're looking at.

MATERIALS

Two identical small objects (like small tempera paint pots or spools of thread)
Yardstick
Pencil

Look at an object in the distance. Then put your hand over one eye and look at the object. Now look at it with your hand over the other eye instead. Did the object seem to move? To "see" this more clearly, place the two identical objects on your desk with one of them slightly farther back than the other. Step back a few feet and squat down so the desk is at eye level. Look at the two objects. Try to touch the one farthest away with the yardstick. Now close one eye and try to touch it. Try it with the other eye closed. It's harder to determine the distance to that object with one of your eyes closed. You've lost some of your depth perception.

You use one of your eyes more than the other. You can figure out which is your dominant eye by looking at an object in the distance. Hold a pencil in your fist at arm's length and line it up with that object while looking at it with both eyes. Close one eye, then open it. Close the other eye, then open it. With one of your eyes closed, the pencil may appear to jump a little away from the object. With the other, it will jump farther. The eye that is closed when the pencil jumps the greatest distance is your dominant eye.

Designs for these inventions were found in Leonardo's notebooks. Some of them weren't invented by others until hundreds of years later.

- Tank
- Helicopter
- Diving suit
- Bicycle
- Submarine
- Hang glider
- An automobile driven by springs
- Parachute
- Explosive shells fired by cannon
- Locks to control the flow of water in canals
- Multi-barreled missile launchers
- Rolling mills for sheet iron
- Mechanical saws and drills
- Pulleys, cranes, drills, bridges, excavators, water turbines, and countless other machines

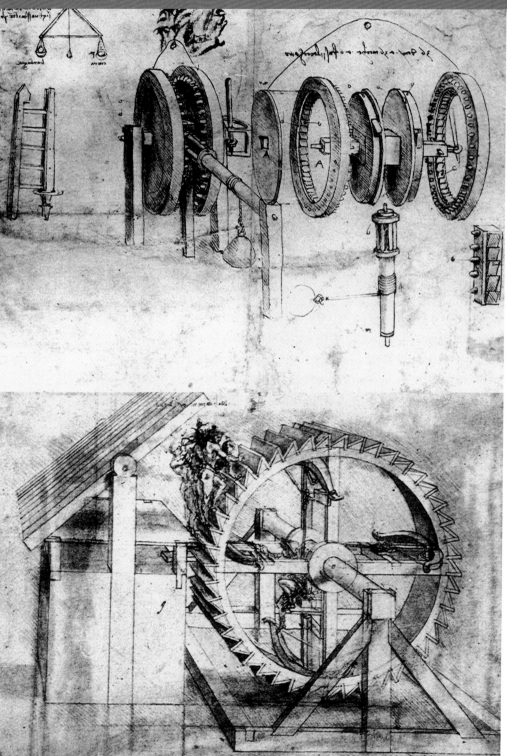

Top: Sketch of parts of a machine, Leonardo da Vinci, 1480

Bottom: Sketch of treadmill crossbow, Leonardo da Vinci, 1488

43

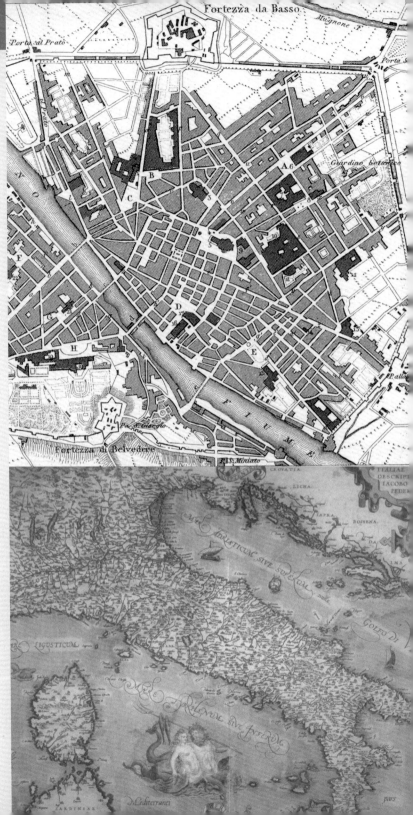

Italy did not become a unified country until 1870. During Leonardo's time it was broken into warring city-states, duchies, kingdoms, and republics ruled by powerful families.

In the south of Italy was the Kingdom of Naples. The Papal States in central Italy were ruled by the pope. In the north were the wealthy city-states including the Duchy of Milan, the Republic of Venice, the Republic of Genoa, and the Republic of Florence, among others.

Italian cities were important centers of trade. They were located conveniently between Greece, North Africa, the countries to the Far East, and the rest of Europe. This trade brought the cities great wealth and power, creating a class of wealthy merchants, bankers, and financiers. Genoa, Pisa, Venice, Milan, and Florence were great centers. Florence was one of the largest cities at this time. Its merchants specialized in beautifully dyed cloth.

Eventually the rulers of the cities came to rule over the people of the surrounding regions. These city-states were often at war with one another and there was constant feuding and violence. Towns such as Florence were built like fortresses, with high walls to stop invaders. People even fortified their homes with towers so they could shoot arrows or pour hot tar on their enemies from above.

Some of the city-states were republics, governed by elected councils. Only the wealthy people, however, were allowed to vote and serve on the councils. Some of the city-states were ruled by rich and powerful families like the Medicis. The Medici family owned the largest bank in Florence. Their customers included the popes and the kings of France.

Top: Detail of the city of Florence

Bottom: Map of Italy, 1600

Because the Medicis and the other wealthy people of this time wanted to be surrounded by beautiful things, they supported many artists. Lorenzo the Magnificent and Ludovico Sforza were rulers of city-states who became patrons of artists including Leonardo and Michelangelo.

When he revealed his design for the Sforza monument there was great excitement in the city. He had a clay model of the horse set up in the "piazza," or courtyard, in the center of the castle and unveiled it to the court's amazement. The horse alone, without the rider, was twenty feet high.

At the same time that he was working on the monument, Leonardo was assigned to design new buildings and watercourses. He had so much work, and it took him so long to finish anything, that Ludovico despaired of Leonardo ever finishing the statue. But soon Ludovico had other things to worry about.

Trouble was brewing in Milan. Ludovico's nephew Gian and his wife, Isabella, were unhappy. Ludovico refused to give Gian his rightful place as ruler of Milan. Isabella wrote to her grandfather, the powerful king of Naples, to complain. The king of Naples prepared his troops to go to war with Milan. And along with the trouble in his own family, there were rumors that France was about to invade the region. For the moment, Ludovico allied himself with the king of France against the other rulers of the Italian city-states, but it was an uneasy alliance.

Although Leonardo's livelihood depended on the wealthy families that supported him, he paid little attention to their concerns. He had plenty of work. He had good living quar-

Study for the head of St. Anne, Leonardo da Vinci, 1508–10

45

Leonardo was a vegetarian. Try this recipe for delicious vegetarian minestrone soup, his favorite meal. You should have all your ingredients ready before you begin to cook. Adult supervision is recommended for this activity. Makes 6 servings.

INGREDIENTS

3 tablespoons olive oil

1 clove garlic, minced

1 small onion, minced

2 medium zucchini, diced

2 carrots, peeled and diced

1/4 pound green beans, ends cut off and cut into thirds

1/4 cup chopped parsley

1/2 teaspoon dried basil

1/2 teaspoon dried oregano

1/2 teaspoon salt

1/4 teaspoon pepper

1 can (16 ounces) red kidney beans, drained

1 can (16 ounces) whole tomatoes, drained and cut into quarters

2 1/2 cups water

3/4 cup elbow macaroni, uncooked

1/4 cup tomato paste

UTENSILS

Measuring spoons and cups

Knife

Large pot

Wooden spoon

Put olive oil in a large pot over medium heat. Add garlic and onion to pot. Cook, stirring occasionally, for ten minutes. Add zucchini, carrots, green beans, parsley, basil, oregano, salt, and pepper. Stir. Add kidney beans, mashing some of them slightly. Add tomatoes and water. Bring to a boil over medium heat. Lower the heat, cover the pot, and simmer for an hour, stirring occasionally. Add macaroni and tomato paste. Simmer fifteen minutes, stirring occasionally. Pass around the "pane" (bread) and enjoy!

ters and a busy workshop, many friends and apprentices, servants, and horses.

Leonardo loved all animals. He often purchased birds at the open-air market only to set them free from their cages. He loved to watch them fly away. He was so fond of animals that he became a vegetarian and lived on a diet of vegetables, fruit, and pasta. He adopted many creatures and cared for them.

Leonardo also adopted a young boy. Giacomo, the son of a poor peasant, was ten years old when he came to stay at Leonardo's bottega. Though he was just a small boy he caused the artist and his assistants a great deal of trouble. As soon as he arrived, Leonardo had a tailor make him several shirts and a jacket. He put aside some money to pay the tailor and when he turned away it disappeared. At dinner that night Giacomo broke three glasses and knocked over the wine. As the days and weeks continued the boy stole money and art supplies and caused trouble wherever he went. Whenever something was missing, it could be found in Giacomo's trunk. He stole a piece of leather Leonardo was saving for boots and sold it for some sweets made of anise seeds. In his notebook, Leonardo wrote that the child "eats supper for two and does mischief for four." Leonardo nicknamed the boy "Salai," meaning demon, but he was fond of him and kept him in his household, took him everywhere, and gave him every-

All of his life, Leonardo loved birds. He studied and drew them. He dreamed of flying like one. You can help birds by volunteering to work on habitat restoration or by providing food and water for the birds in your own backyard. Be sure to get permission from an adult before turning your backyard into a bird sanctuary. Adult supervision is recommended for this activity.

MATERIALS

Large, shallow bowl or terra-cotta drainage tray from the bottom of a large planter

1 cup lard, suet, or bacon drippings

1 cup birdseed

1/2 cup sunflower seeds

1/4 cup cornmeal

Crushed shells of 2 eggs

1/4 cup nuts, chopped

1 tin can (16 ounce size), empty and rinsed out

1 piece of string, 10 inches long

Medium pot

Can opener

Notebook

Pen

Bird guidebook (optional)

Pencils

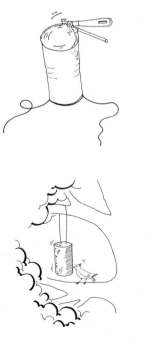

Birds need water to drink and to keep their feathers clean. Provide a bath by placing a shallow bowl in a quiet corner of your yard. Fill it with fresh water every day.

Birds need dinner, too! Melt 1 cup of the lard, suet, or bacon drippings over low heat. Set it aside for 30 minutes to cool. Stir the birdseed, the sunflower seeds, cornmeal, crushed eggshells, and nuts into the melted fat. Place the 10-inch length of string in a loop in the tin can and pour the mixture around it. Place the can in the refrigerator. When the mixture has hardened, remove the bottom of the can with a can opener and push the mixture through. Hang this yummy meal from a tree branch.

In your discovery notebook, record the birds that come to feed and bathe in your yard. Try to identify the birds that come to visit using your bird guide. Note the time of year they are visiting your feeder. Sketch the birds you see.

thing. He tried to teach the boy to paint. Salai became an apprentice painter and was also Leonardo's cherished and indulged son.

Leonardo's mother, Caterina, was a widow now and not well. Leonardo invited her into his home and she stayed with him in Milan until she died.

Leonardo's notebooks were crowded with all of his interests. He traveled to the Alps and became one of the earliest mountaineers, climbing the high peak of Monte Rosa. At the summit he looked down on the clouds, the glaciers, and the streams running through the canyons. Leonardo was thrilled to see the landscape from a "vista d'uccello," a bird's-eye view. When he saw what appeared to be seashells on the slopes of the mountains he guessed that they were the remains (fossils) of once-living sea creatures and that the land where the mountain now stood had at one time been covered by the sea. He noticed that the hillsides were made of layers of rock and became the first to figure out the theory of sedimentation. This theory stated that these layers were formed over time and that the oldest rocks were at the bottom. He speculated on the intense blue sky overhead and was the first to conclude that the sky's color was due to light reflected by small particles in the air.

The mountain streams fascinated Leonardo and he carefully observed the flow

Study of cats and dragon, Leonardo da Vinci, 1513–14

48

of water around rocks and the movement of objects in the water. His interest in the forces of water led him to think about ways to harness its energy. Back in his workshop he designed waterwheels, mills, locks, and canals.

He continued his work on the Sforza monument. He also designed machines for spinning and weaving. For Ludovico's pleasure, Leonardo decorated a room at the castle, the "Sala dell' Asse," Hall of the Axis. He painted tree trunks growing up from the baseboard and greenery all around the walls. A blue sky peeked through the tree leaves and a golden ribbon wound in and out of the grove. Also during this time, Leonardo decided that he wanted to be able to read scholarly books. Back then, books were written in Latin and Leonardo only knew a dialect of Italian. He set out to teach himself the language, writing down passages in Latin in his notebooks and keeping notes of new words and definitions.

Leonardo found a friend in a monk and mathematician named Luca Pacioli. Luca was compiling a work of all mathematical knowledge. Soon Leonardo's notebooks were full of mathematical equations and geometrical games. Together he and Luca created a book, called *De Divina Proportione*.

Leonardo had an insatiable curiosity. He questioned everything. When he was a boy, he constantly pulled on his Uncle

Anise, an herb of the carrot family, has a sweet, licorice taste. It's been popular with Italian bakers since the Roman Empire. Salai found the taste especially irresistible. Adult supervision is recommended for this activity.

INGREDIENTS

- ½ cup butter or margarine, softened
- ½ cup confectioners' sugar
- 1 cup flour
- 1 teaspoon anise seeds, crushed
- 1 cup pitted dates, cut up into small pieces
- 1 cup raisins
- 1½ cups water

UTENSILS

- Medium-sized bowl
- Hand mixer
- Oblong pan, 13 by 9 ½
- by 2 inches
- Wooden spoon
- Spatula
- Saucepan

Preheat oven to 350 degrees. Place butter or margarine in bowl of mixer. Add confectioners' sugar. Beat until smooth with hand mixer. Scrape the batter from the sides of the bowl with a spatula. Add flour and mix in. Place mixture into the oblong pan and pat it down evenly with your hand. Bake fifteen minutes. Remove from the oven and let cool.

Crush the anise seeds by placing them on a board and grinding them with the bottom of a wooden spoon. Place the dates, raisins, anise seeds, and water in a saucepan. Cook, stirring, over low heat for 10 minutes. (The mixture will thicken.) Remove from the heat and let cool for 10 minutes. Spread the topping over the crust. Chill in the refrigerator for 2 hours. Cut into squares and eat!

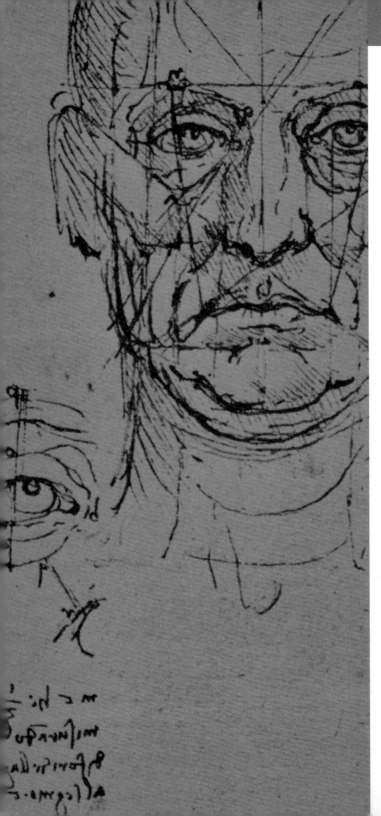

Many of us are good at some things, like math and science, or drawing, or writing. But Leonardo did so many things. It seems almost impossible that one person could have accomplished them all. How did he do it?

It may have had something to do with the way his mind worked. Leonardo was able to focus his mind entirely on the subject in front of him, but he was also able to open his mind and find connections between all of his studies. He used his whole brain: intuition and logic, imagination and observation. He let himself dream while he trained his mind to study. Here are some of the exercises Leonardo used to strengthen his mind:

- **To stimulate the imagination**—"In order to excite the mind, contemplate walls covered with shapeless stains or made of ill-assorted stones. Find in them mountain landscapes, trees, battles, figures with lively movements, faces, and strange costumes."

- **To train the memory**—Leonardo called this way of looking "knowing how to see." He suggested artists "begin with a detail and only move from one detail to another when you have fixed the first firmly in your memory and become well acquainted with it." He thought the mind of a painter should be like a mirror.

- **To expand ideas**—Leonardo questioned everything. When he read a book, he kept a notebook nearby and wrote down words and passages. He wrote down ideas the book gave him and drew pictures it brought to mind.

Before he went to sleep at night, Leonardo would go over everything he'd worked on that day. He wrote in his notebooks, "I have found that it is of no small benefit when you lie in bed in the dark to go over again in the imagination the outlines of the forms you have been studying; this is certainly a praiseworthy exercise and useful in impressing things on the memory."

Sketch of human proportions,
Leonardo da Vinci, 1488–89

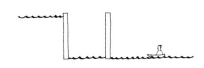

Leonardo spent a lot of time thinking about water. As an engineer he realized it was an important source of power. Also, in Leonardo's time, people and products traveled by water—it was much easier than hauling goods by horse or donkey along the roads of that time. Leonardo designed canals (man-made waterways), machines powered by waterwheels, and an innovative lock and dam system.

A lock is used to help boats travel when there is a change in elevation along a canal. It's an enclosed part of a canal or waterway. At each end of the lock there is a gate that can be opened and shut. The level of the water inside the lock is raised or lowered so that boats can continue to travel up or down the canal. When a boat approaches a lock, the lower gate opens, then closes behind it. Valves let water in from the top and the boat rises until it is at the same elevation as the water beyond the top lock. The top gate is then opened and the boat travels on.

Leonardo invented special locks around 1500 and they are still in use today! His design has two gates that close in a V-shape. He designed them so that the force of the water keeps them closed.

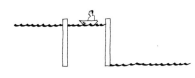

Study for the
dome of the Milan
cathedral,
Leonardo da Vinci,
1488

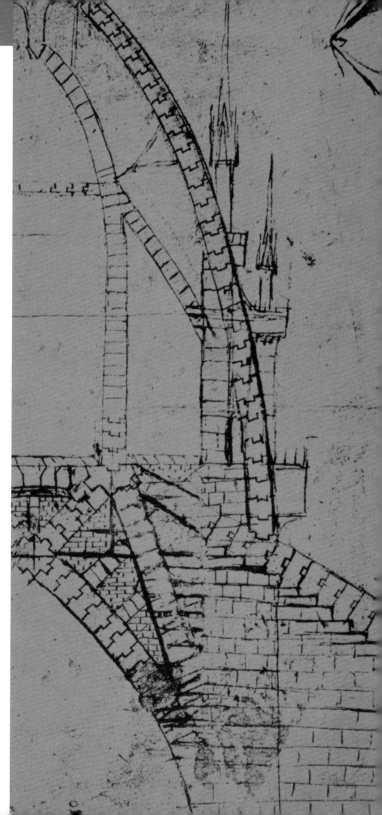

Studies for a domed church,
Leonardo da Vinci, 1485–90

Learn a Little Italian

Teach yourself a few words of Italian every day. It's easy as uno, due, tre.

English	Italian	How to say it
Good morning.	Buon giorno.	BWON JORno
Good night.	Buona notte.	BWONno Nawtte
My name is.	Mi chiamo.	MEE kyahMO
How are you?	Come stai?	KOme STY
Fine, thank you.	Bene, grazie.	BEne, GRAHtzee
So long.	Ciao.	CHAHo
Excuse me.	Scusa.	SCOOzah
Please.	Per favore.	PEYR faVORay
Thank you very much.	Mille grazie.	MEELle GRAHtzee
Yes	Si	SEE
No	No	NO
One	Uno	OONO
Two	Due	DOOwe
Three	Tre	TREY
Four	Quattro	KWAHTtro
Five	Cinque	CHEENkwe
Six	Sei	SEYee
Seven	Sette	SEYTte
Eight	Otto	AWTto
Nine	Nove	NAWve
Ten	Dieci	DEE-Eychee

Francesco's sleeve, saying, "Tell me." Now he asked his friends for answers to his many questions. He wrote notes to himself to remember to "Ask Giannino how the tower of Ferrara was built," "Ask Benedetto how people travel on ice in Flanders," "Get the master of mathematics to show me how to square a triangle."

More than anything, Leonardo wanted to understand flight. For hours at a time, he watched birds in flight, studying the movements of their wings and the ways they moved to catch the currents of the wind. He made models of their wings and the wings of bats. He tested different materials to use for a flying machine. He barricaded the top rooms of his bottega so he could make large models in secret. He made hundreds of designs and called them all "uccello," bird. One of his designs used canvas covered with feathers. Another had wings made of leather and cane and starched silk that were nearly eighty feet long. He made a model of a helicopter and also designed a parachute.

All of his life Leonardo had watched birds and sketched them and dreamed of seeing the world from a bird's-eye view. He began to think of trying out his machines himself and looked for suitable rooftops in Milan. He wanted to try to fly from the roof of his workshop and wrote, "Tomorrow morning I shall make the attempt." But it must not have worked. In his next reference to the attempt at flight he cautions himself to "experiment over a lake wearing an empty wineskin as a belt so that if you fall in you will not be drowned."

Leonardo had to set aside his dreams of flying for yet another project. The monks of Santa Maria delle Grazie asked Ludovico for the services of a painter to decorate a wall of their dining hall, called a "refectory." Ludovico gave Leonardo the assignment of painting *The Last Supper* (see page 56).

As usual, Leonardo started his work by making sketches. The arrangement of Christ and his apostles along the long table would require careful composition. Leonardo designed the work so that the viewer's eyes would be drawn to the head of Christ. He wanted the figures in the painting to give the viewer a sense of both balance and movement.

Leonardo wanted to tell the story of the Last Supper through the gestures of the apostles. He chose to show the moment when Christ said, "One of you will betray me." In the painting, each apostle reacts in a different way. Some express shock, some fear, some anger, some disbelief. Leonardo wanted to reveal the feelings and thoughts of each of them through their postures and gestures and facial expressions. He felt the painter's task was to paint the man and his soul. In *The Last Supper* he accomplished this perfectly.

Just as iron rusts from disuse . . . so our intellect wastes unless it is kept in use.

—Leonardo

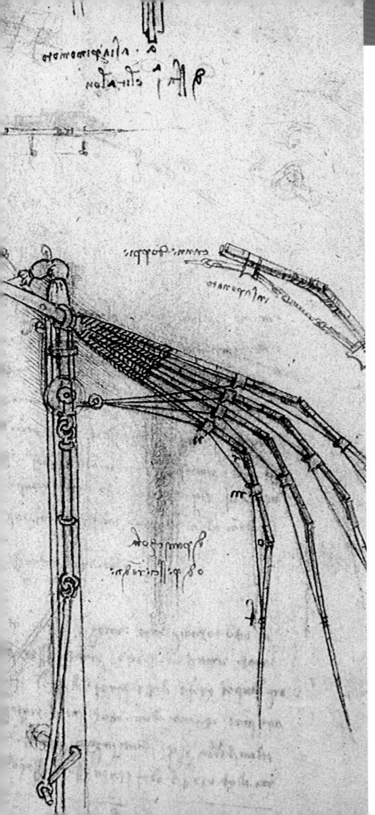

Did you ever wonder how something heavier than air can fly? Leonardo did. He was obsessed with flight and spent decades studying birds and designing flying machines. It wasn't until hundreds of years later, in 1903, that the Wright brothers achieved powered flight.

Airplanes fly because they are held up by air. But how can this be if an egg, which is much lighter than an airplane, falls to the ground (and goes splat) when you release it? The secret is in the shape and positioning of the airplane's wings.

If you look at the wing of an airplane, you will see that the top is curved and the bottom flat. This shape is called an "airfoil." When the powerful engine propels the plane forward, this causes air to rush across the wings. The wing's special airfoil shape causes the air moving over the top of the wing to move faster than the air moving under it. The faster-moving air on top of the wing presses on the wing more lightly than the slower-moving air passing below. The difference in the pressure on the top and the bottom generates "lift," which overcomes the force of gravity, allowing the plane to climb and stay aloft.

You can feel how lift works by putting your hand out the window of a fast-moving car. If you keep your hand flat, it stays flat. But if you tilt your hand up slightly, it lifts up into the air. You can also see lift work when you fly a kite. Run with a kite behind you and notice how the air pushes against the surface of the kite and lifts it up. The faster you run (you are the power source, like the thrust of an airplane engine), the higher the kite will lift.

Diagram of a flying machine,
Leonardo da Vinci, 1486–90

Here's a kite based on Leonardo's drawing of a parachute.

16-inch square piece of plastic (you can
   use a cut-up plastic garbage bag)
Scissors
Kite string
Ruler
Darning needle
Small toy figure
Ribbon, 1 inch wide by 2 feet long

Cut a ½-inch round hole in the center of the plastic. Cut 3 pieces of string into 12-inch lengths. With the darning needle, draw one piece of string through the plastic at one of the corners. Make a knot at one end of the string, as shown in the illustration. Do the same with the two other pieces of string at two other corners. Pull the three pieces of string together and tie them in a knot. You can tie a small toy figure (the parachutist!) to this spot. Then tie the end of your kite string to the knot, too. Cut another piece of string into a 6-inch length and thread it through the fourth corner in 2 places, as shown. Tie the ribbon to this piece of string to make the kite's tail.

Take your kite out on a windy day. Unwind about 1 yard of the kite string, and let your parachute kite catch the breeze. Run into the wind to help your kite gain lift and let the string out as it climbs.

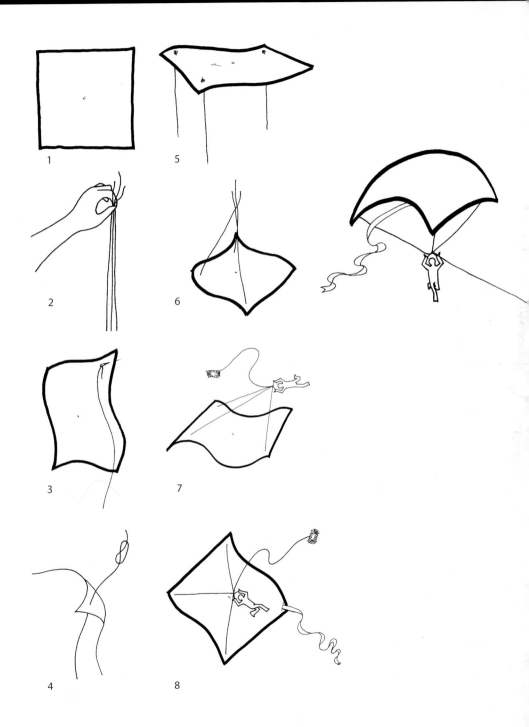

The Last Supper
Leonardo da Vinci,
1495–98

Leonardo would sometimes appear at the refectory at sunrise and paint until dark without ever once putting down his brush to eat or drink. On other days he would simply stand in front of his work for hours with his arms folded. Sometimes he could be seen racing down the streets to the monastery where he would grab a brush, climb up the scaffolding, add a couple of brushstrokes to the mural, and abruptly leave. Sometimes weeks would go by and he wouldn't show up at all.

The monks didn't understand how a man could work in this way. They were getting tired of having their refectory filled with paints and scaffolding. But even though Leonardo didn't work on the painting every day, he thought about it constantly. He walked the streets staring at people, looking for ideas for the faces of the apostles. He sat in cafes and watched people, observing their movements and facial expressions and sketching them in his notebook. He looked for expressions of surprise, pain, fear, and anger and noted which facial muscles worked to express these feelings. He used the faces of people he saw on the streets of Milan in his work.

Finally, the painting was complete, with the exception of the head of Judas. Leonardo walked the

Top left: Study for *The Last Supper*, Leonardo da Vinci, 1497

Top right: Study for *The Battle of Anghirari*, Leonardo da Vinci, 1503–04

Bottom left: Old man with oak leaves and caricatures, Leonardo da Vinci, late 1490s

Bottom right: Study of an old man, Leonardo da Vinci, 1500

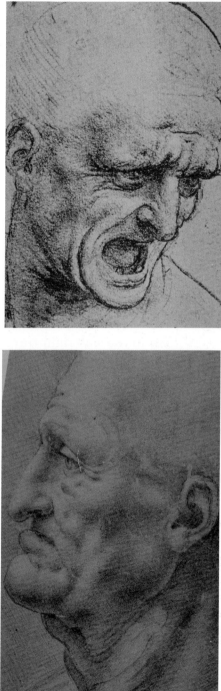

Leonardo liked to try new methods and new paints. When he painted *The Last Supper* on the wall of the refectory at Santa Maria delle Grazie, he wanted to try something different.

Other artists at this time might have used the traditional technique known as fresco. In this technique, layers of plaster were spread over the walls and then colors mixed with water were painted onto the plaster while it was still wet. Artists using this technique had to work very quickly and mistakes were difficult to correct once the plaster dried.

Leonardo liked to work slowly, so he used a combination of oil, varnish, and pigments on dry plaster. He spent three years painting *The Last Supper*, but within twenty years the experimental paint started to flake off.

Just decades after he painted it, *The Last Supper* was retouched by other artists who were not as talented as Leonardo. Then the monks cut a door in the wall right through part of the painting. The room was flooded twice. When Napoleon's troops were in Milan, they used the refectory as a stable for their horses and threw bricks at the painting. During World War II the building was bombed and almost entirely destroyed.

The Last Supper has been cleaned and restored many times. Early on, painters simply painted over Leonardo's figures with oil paints. Others attempted to glue paint fragments that had fallen to the ground back on the painting. The latest restoration effort was begun in the late seventies and has just recently been completed. Restorers carefully stripped the painting of the layers of paint applied during previous restoration efforts. They cleaned off years of mold and grime and soot. They used x ray, infrared, and ultraviolet sensors to figure out which layers of paint were applied by Leonardo and which by other painters. These restorers reversed much of the damage *The Last Supper* has seen over the years.

Detail of *The Last Supper*,
Leonardo da Vinci, 1495–98

streets looking for an appropriate face for the man who had betrayed Jesus. He frequented jails and the most dangerous parts of the city. Months were passing by and the monks were growing impatient and angry. The head monk went to Ludovico to complain. "Basta! Enough! Tell this artist to finish his work!" he said to Ludovico. Ludovico told Leonardo about the head monk's complaints. But Leonardo would not be hurried. He suggested that if the head monk would like the face of Judas finished right away that the monk serve as the model for Judas the betrayer. The monk's complaints were silenced.

And when the painting was finished they knew it was worth any inconvenience. People came from everywhere to see it. Artists brought sketchbooks and copied it so they could use Leonardo's ideas.

It wasn't unusual for Leonardo to take a long time to create a painting. Often he didn't finish his work. He didn't even pick up a brush until he had given careful thought to what he wanted to do. For months he would create the painting in his mind, make sketches, and calculate the placement of figures. Many of his patrons grew impatient with Leonardo.

Leonardo spent years working on *The Last Supper*, but shortly after he finished it the painting began to disintegrate. He often experimented with different paints and

techniques and he had done so with this work. Sometimes he made paints with walnut oil, sometimes with the oil of the cypress tree. He made paints with honey, with eggs, and with various resins. Normally a painting such as this one would have been done in fresco, but that method required speed and Leonardo liked to work slowly. The mixture he used for *The Last Supper* did not last and the paint began flaking off the wall of the refectory.

With *The Last Supper* complete, Leonardo once again turned his attention to the bronze statue for Ludovico. But this work was never to be finished. For once, this was through no fault of Leonardo's. Ludovico was at war with the king of Naples, who was angry at the slight to Isabella, and the king of France had crossed the Alps with his troops. Milan was threatened. The bronze Leonardo was to have used for the statue was made into cannons to use for war. The statue Leonardo spent so much time preparing to create would never be made.

Statues and paintings were not very important to Ludovico now. Instead he wanted weapons and defense works for his city. Leonardo designed a giant catapult, over seventy feet long, made with special firing mechanisms and designed so that it could be operated in complete silence. He invented a tank with special hand cranks that would allow the men inside to move and turn it quickly. He created a terrifying chariot with turning blades that no enemy could get near.

Ludovico poisoned his nephew Gian and declared himself the official Duke of Milan. But his reign was short-lived. The armies of France invaded Italy and city after city fell before them. Though Ludovico had once allied himself with the king of France, he broke that alliance and joined the other Italian rulers to fight against the invaders.

It did him little good. King Louis XII and his French army invaded Milan. Ludovico fled the city with his family and his fortune. Milan became a French city and the invading army took over its streets. The soldiers entertained themselves by shooting arrows at Leonardo's clay horse. King Louis thought *The Last Supper* so magnificent he wanted to move the wall it was painted on to his palace in France.

With his patron Ludovico gone, Leonardo felt unsafe in the city he had called his home for the last eighteen years. In September of 1499 he packed three bags and, with his friend Luca Pacioli, his assistant Tommaso, and the young Salai, he hurriedly left Milan.

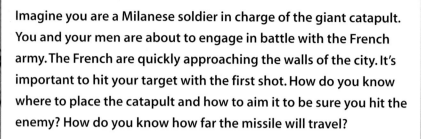

Imagine you are a Milanese soldier in charge of the giant catapult. You and your men are about to engage in battle with the French army. The French are quickly approaching the walls of the city. It's important to hit your target with the first shot. How do you know where to place the catapult and how to aim it to be sure you hit the enemy? How do you know how far the missile will travel?

The catapult can hurl a missile (a 40-pound boulder!) at a speed of 60 miles per hour. Leonardo has designed the catapult so you can vary the direction of travel (the launch angle) the missile takes. When the launch angle is high, the missile tends to go up fairly high but it doesn't travel very far. If you lower the angle, the missile travels farther.

The French get closer! Start calculating!

distance = speed x speed x flight factor

You know the speed of the missile (60 miles per hour) and you are setting the launch angle on the catapult. All you need is the flight factor, which will vary with each launch angle.

Angle	Flight Factor	Angle	Flight Factor
10 degrees	0.023	45 degrees	0.0672
30 degrees	0.0582	60 degrees	0.0582

We can see the banners of the French army! Their armor glints in the sunlight! The pounding of the horses' hooves reaches our ears!

Quick—look up the flight factor in the table. Use that number and the speed in the formula. How far will the missile travel if we set the launch angle for 30 degrees?

distance = 60 x 60 x 0.0582 *or* distance = 209.52 feet

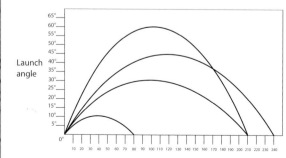

Launch angle

This missile will fall short of the enemy, now 250 feet away. Try the other flight angles to see if any of them will hit your target.

FOUR

"I shall continue."

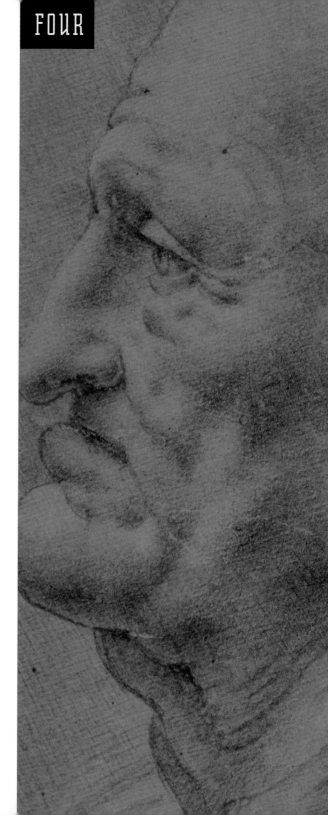

It seemed that all of the cities of Italy were at war, either with the French or with one another, and Leonardo did not know where to turn. Though he designed weapons and fortifications and served under the battling rulers, he thought war was a "bestialissima pazzia," a bestial madness.

For a while he stayed in Mantua, with Isabella d'Este, Ludovico's sister-in-law. Isabella was a great patroness of the arts, and a woman who was used to getting her way. She owned paintings by all the famous artists of the time and it was her greatest wish to have her portrait done by Leonardo. He drew a profile of her in pencil and chalk, telling her that he would someday paint it in oil. But he didn't care for the tyrannical woman and left her estate for the city of Venice.

When he reached Venice he heard that his old patron, Ludovico, had tried to reconquer Milan. Ludovico briefly recaptured his city only to lose it again to the French. He tried to escape by disguising himself as a common soldier, but was recognized and taken to France where he was imprisoned. Ludovico spent the rest of his life in captivity. Leonardo wrote of his patron's fate in his notebooks, along with the troubles of his other friends in Milan who were ruined by the war.

Fighting was also going on in Venice, which was threatened by an invasion of the Turkish army. The city's leaders knew of Leonardo's reputation and asked for his help as a military advisor. He suggested a lock and dam that would allow the Venetians to flood an entire valley and

Study of an old man, Leonardo da Vinci, 1500

drown the enemy army of Turks. Leonardo had also invented a diving suit that would enable men to swim underwater beneath the enemy ships so they could pierce and sink them. But in his notebooks, he wrote that he should not reveal the secret of this diving suit to anyone. He didn't want to see the crews of ships all going to the bottom of the sea because of his invention.

Leonardo left Venice for his old home of Florence. He found it a different city from the one he had left so many years ago. Lorenzo was dead and the Medici family was no longer in power. Maestro Verrocchio was also dead. But Leonardo's father was still there. Seventy-four years old, he lived with his fourth wife, Lucrezia di Guglielmo, and his eleven other children.

The Florentines were pleased to have the famous artist back in their city. Some monks gave him and Salai and Luca a place to stay in their monastery. Leonardo helped to restore a church and designed a villa for a rich patron. He became fascinated with the properties of percussion at this time and conducted experiments on sound. He and Luca stayed up late at night studying mathematics.

Leonardo also received a commission from the monks for a painting. This painting was *The Virgin and Child with Saint Anne.* His preliminary drawing for the painting astonished the townspeople. The drawing hung on display, and for two days people filed

Drawing for
*The Virgin and
Child with Saint
Anne,* Leonardo
da Vinci, 1498

through and looked at it in awestruck silence. The entwined figures and sweet expressions were marvelous. But again, Leonardo did not finish the painting, although he continued to work on it for years.

In this summer of 1502, Cesare Borgia came to find Leonardo to hire him as his military engineer. Leonardo had met Cesare Borgia when the French invaded Milan. Borgia assisted the French in conquering that city and they rewarded him with an army and a French title, Duke of Valentinois. Borgia, a bloodthirsty warrior, wanted to conquer all of central Italy.

As military engineer, Leonardo traveled throughout central Italy, visiting all the towns under Borgia's command. The Duke wanted him to examine all of the castles and fortresses he'd captured to be sure they were prepared for war. In each town, Leonardo studied the walls and suggested improvements for fortifications. He devised canals, reservoirs, ramparts, and moats. Everywhere he went, he pursued his own interests as well. At a town on the seacoast, while he planned fortifications and techniques to drain marshes, he studied the movements of the waves and tides. When Borgia's troops invaded another small town, Leonardo immediately went in search of its books. In yet another town, he sketched a particularly interesting staircase

Top: Sketch of Castello Sforzesco, Leonardo da Vinci, 1497

Bottom: Sketch of treadmill crossbow, Leonardo da Vinci, 1488

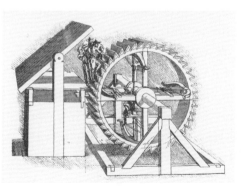

The Nature of Sound

Leonardo was the first to suggest that sound travels in waves. Just like ripples spread out in a pond when you throw a rock into it, sound travels in waves from its source outward. Imagine a series of waves coming out of your stereo speakers—when they reach your ear, you hear the sound.

The speed at which the waves travel is called the "frequency". When waves travel very quickly (high frequency) the sounds are higher; slower waves (low frequency) are lower.

Paintings are bought, sold, given away, stolen, lost, and found. They end up in unlikely places sometimes. Art historians have to be like detectives to trace the history of a painting and to spot forgeries.

Sometimes there is a written record for important works of art, like the original contract for the piece, a mention in an inventory of a church, or in a will left by a wealthy person who owned the artwork. But sometimes paintings are simply lost in the shuffle of history. One of Leonardo's paintings, *The Benois Madonna*, disappeared for three hundred years then turned up in the possession of a traveling musician. He sold it to a man who left it to his children when he died. They gave it to a museum, the Hermitage, in Russia.

Another work, the painting *Saint Jerome*, was also lost for centuries. One day a cardinal, an official from the Roman Catholic Church, was walking down a street in Rome and looked into the window of a shop. He noticed a cupboard with an interesting painting on it, the head of Saint Jerome. The cardinal thought it looked important, so he bought the cupboard and found out it was a painting by Leonardo. He spent the next few months searching the city for the rest of the painting. He finally found the painting—it had been turned into a shoemaker's bench! The cardinal bought that as well and put the painting back together. Today it hangs in the Vatican in Rome.

When the *Mona Lisa* was stolen from the Louvre in Paris (see page 70), several forgeries appeared around the world. They were so good that people bought them thinking they were buying the original *Mona Lisa*. Curators and art historians must learn the techniques of artists down to the smallest brush strokes so they can tell if they have an original or a forgery.

Detail of *Saint Jerome*, Leonardo da Vinci, 1480

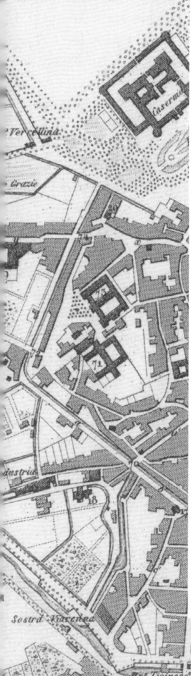

When Leonardo became a military engineer for Cesare Borgia he created many maps. Mapmakers are also called "cartographers." Leonardo was one of the first cartographers to draw maps from a vista d'uccello, a bird's-eye view.

MATERIALS

Stick, at least 8 inches long
Maps to use as examples
Sheet of paper, 8 ½ by 11 inches
Pencil
Ruler

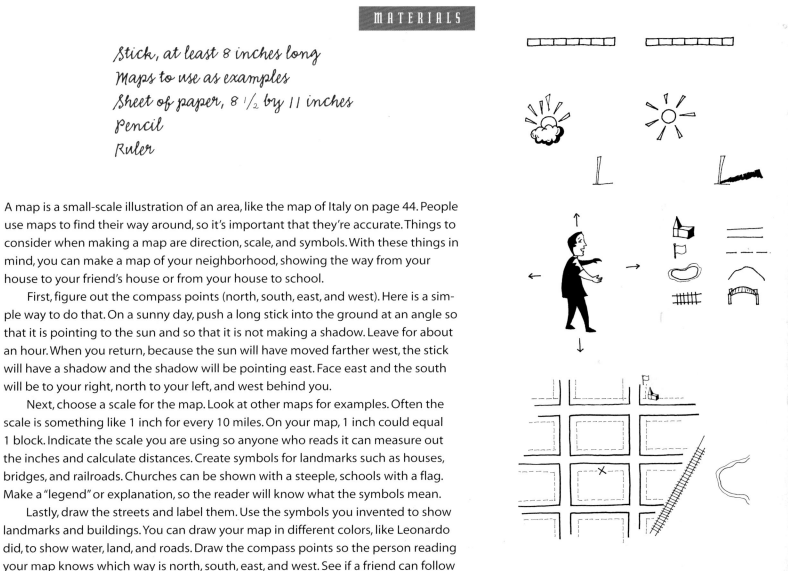

A map is a small-scale illustration of an area, like the map of Italy on page 44. People use maps to find their way around, so it's important that they're accurate. Things to consider when making a map are direction, scale, and symbols. With these things in mind, you can make a map of your neighborhood, showing the way from your house to your friend's house or from your house to school.

First, figure out the compass points (north, south, east, and west). Here is a simple way to do that. On a sunny day, push a long stick into the ground at an angle so that it is pointing to the sun and so that it is not making a shadow. Leave for about an hour. When you return, because the sun will have moved farther west, the stick will have a shadow and the shadow will be pointing east. Face east and the south will be to your right, north to your left, and west behind you.

Next, choose a scale for the map. Look at other maps for examples. Often the scale is something like 1 inch for every 10 miles. On your map, 1 inch could equal 1 block. Indicate the scale you are using so anyone who reads it can measure out the inches and calculate distances. Create symbols for landmarks such as houses, bridges, and railroads. Churches can be shown with a steeple, schools with a flag. Make a "legend" or explanation, so the reader will know what the symbols mean.

Lastly, draw the streets and label them. Use the symbols you invented to show landmarks and buildings. You can draw your map in different colors, like Leonardo did, to show water, land, and roads. Draw the compass points so the person reading your map knows which way is north, south, east, and west. See if a friend can follow your map.

Leonardo liked to test his perceptions by guessing distances and heights. When he was walking he would pick an object in the distance and estimate the number of paces it would take to walk to it. He tried to guess the heights of buildings and trees. It was good practice for painting and mapmaking. But how could he tell if he was right? Pick a tree, guess its height, and use this technique to measure it.

MATERIALS

Stick, at least 8 inches long
Measuring tape

On a sunny day, push a stick into the ground so that 6 inches of it shows. Measure the length of the stick's shadow. Measure the length of the shadow cast by the tree you picked. Then use a simple equation to calculate the height of the tree.

In this example, the shadow of the stick is 10 inches long and the shadow of the tree is 360 inches long. You would calculate the tree's height in this way:

Multiply the height of the stick (6 inches) by the length of the tree's shadow (360 inches). This equals 2,160 inches. Divide that by the length of the stick's shadow (10 inches). That number, 216, is the height of your tree in inches. (216 inches = 18 feet)

Written as an equation, it looks like this:

$$\text{Height of tree} = \frac{\text{Height of stick} \times \text{Length of the tree's shadow}}{\text{Length of stick's shadow}}$$

In our example:

$$\text{Height of tree} = \frac{6 \text{ inches} \times 360 \text{ inches}}{10 \text{ inches}}$$
$$= 216 \text{ inches (or 18 feet)}$$

and studied the workings of a fountain. During this time he also designed a windmill and drew a design for a bridge with an arch that was over 780 feet long.

To assist Borgia in his scheme to conquer central Italy, Leonardo drew maps of the region. He paced out distances of roads and open spaces. He drew every road and fortress, wall and gate. He included the buildings in the towns and the surrounding villas. He even color-coded his maps, showing towns in green, the countryside in yellow, and moats and rivers in light blue. His maps were perfectly calculated and drawn. With these, Borgia would know the exact places where he could enter a city and the locations of blind spots and escape routes. They were very useful. Leonardo even included compass bearings and the distances to neighboring towns. The maps helped Borgia to gain control of all of central Italy.

Leonardo hated the wars. Borgia was a cruel and violent man—he'd even ordered the death of his own brother! Leonardo decided to leave Borgia's employment.

In March of 1503, Leonardo, accompanied by Salai, made his way back to Florence. But even there he couldn't escape the fighting, for Florence was at war with the coastal town of Pisa. Leonardo proposed diverting the Arno River so Pisa would no longer have a supply of water and would be forced to surrender peacefully.

In order to carry out the diversion of the large river, Leonardo designed an excavating machine. He might have hated war, but he loved engineering projects. He came up with an idea to create a series of canals so that ships could sail directly to Florence and they wouldn't need to depend on the port town of Pisa for their trade. He devised pumps and locks. He thought the waterway could power sawmills and papermills and other industries. He also designed a circular fortress of three fortified rings surrounded by moats. The walls of his fortress were curved to deflect cannon balls. He drew underground tunnels and bridges that could easily be flooded and destroyed in case of enemy invasion.

Surrounded by war everywhere he turned, it wasn't unusual that Leonardo's next work of art would be of a battle scene. He was hired to create a painting for a wall in the Palazzo Vecchio in Florence and he began work on a scene from the Battle of Anghiari. This was a great battle that had occurred between Florence and Milan in years past which the city wanted to commemorate.

Drawing after Leonardo's *The Battle of Anghiari*, Peter Paul Rubens, 1605

Leonardo drew a scene full of hate and fury. He tried to show the horrors of war in this work. He worked on *The Battle of Anghiari* for three years while the great artist Michelangelo painted a different battle

Look around your house and you will see many machines designed to make your life easier. The kitchen can opener is an obvious one, but pliers are also machines and so are the blinds on the windows. Basically, a machine is a tool to do work. People invent machines to help them push, pull, or lift objects (also thought of as exerting force on objects). There are simple machines and compound machines (those that include two or more simple machines to do the work).

Many of the machines Leonardo invented and sketched in his notebooks were too sophisticated for his time and weren't made until centuries later. But they contained components that were, simply, simple machines.

One simple machine is the inclined plane. An example of this is a ramp. If you are loading boxes onto a truck you will find it is much easier to slide them up a ramp than to lift them up onto the truck bed. The ramp might not look like it, but it's a machine. Another simple machine is the lever. When you use the claw of a hammer to remove a nail from a wall, the hammer is acting as a lever. A pulley is another example of a simple machine. If you have blinds on your windows, you can see how the pulley works. It lifts the blinds up with a cord wrapped around the wheel at the top. Other examples of simple machines are the screw, the wedge, and the wheel and axle. By combining simple machines, Leonardo invented many compound machines, from cranes to catapults.

scene on the wall opposite his. Neither of these works was ever finished. But the partially completed paintings were displayed and artists came from everywhere to see them. Even unfinished, Leonardo's painting had a great impact on the Florentines and the artists who saw it.

In his notebooks Leonardo wrote about the emotions he wanted to show in this work. He wanted to paint the dust and dirt and smoke of battle as well as the terror and agony of death. He said, "Arrows will be flying in all directions. A horse will be dragging behind it the body of its dead rider. Make the vanquished look pale and panic stricken, their eyebrows raised high or knitted in grief, their faces stricken with painfulness . . . The victors wipe their hands over their eyes and cheeks to remove the thick layer of mud caused by their eyes watering on account of the dust." Once again, Leonardo was trying new techniques. For this painting, he layered the plaster wall with tar and used oil paints made with linseed oil.

He was working on *The Battle of Anghiari* when he got the news of his father's death in 1504. He was working on it when he tried again to fly, this time from the top of Monte Ceceri, near Florence. And he was still working on it when he was called back to Milan by the French in 1506. Once again, he left a work unfinished. He had tried to include so much detail and was such a perfectionist that it was difficult for him to bring any work to conclusion.

The French admired the works Leonardo had left in Milan so much that the king's lieutenant, Charles d'Amboise, wrote to the city of Florence requesting Leonardo's presence back in Milan. Leonardo returned to his beloved city. He was welcomed like a returning prince and became once again the center of the community of artists. The lieutenant asked Leonardo to design a palace for him and Leonardo planned one with exotic gardens and pools, citrus trees, flower beds, and an aviary. He designed windmills for the garden that would power musical instruments and a special place where water would suddenly spray out to soak passersby, just for fun. Once again Leonardo was asked to create pageants and entertainments including a special pageant for King Louis XII. He was also asked to work on the canal system and created a new series of locks and dams for the city.

In 1507, Leonardo's Uncle Francesco died and Leonardo needed to return to Florence. He was in Florence for a long time when the French and King Louis became eager for him to return once again to Milan. The two cities began to fight over his presence. Everyone wanted a painting by Leonardo.

As an artist Leonardo was at the peak of his talent. He was now fifty-five years old. It was just a few years earlier that he painted a picture of a woman on a balcony, quietly smiling. He took this painting everywhere with him, working on it for many years. He never wrote about it in his notebooks and left no clue about the identity of the woman in the painting.

The portrait of the woman was incredibly lifelike, from the pores of her skin and the veins in her throat to her delicate eyebrows and glowing eyes. With his brush, Leonardo used a special technique of building up thin layers of paint, giving the painting a radiant quality. And he portrayed Mona Lisa smiling in a mysterious way that would haunt the painting's viewers for centuries to come.

While traveling between Florence and Milan, Leonardo met a young nobleman, Francesco Melzi. They became the best of friends and Melzi joined Leonardo to become his pupil and learn the art of painting. The wealthy, high-born Melzi became Leonardo's assistant. They were to remain together for the rest of Leonardo's life.

The *Mona Lisa* is the most famous painting in the history of art, and it has been reproduced more than any other. Yet no one knows the identity of the woman in the portrait. Though Leonardo left us thousands of pages of notes, he doesn't mention anything about this work.

An early art historian thought it was a painting of Lisa di Gherardini, the third wife of a Florentine silk trader named Francesco del Giocondo. In Italy, the painting is known as *La Gioconda*. Our name for it, *Mona Lisa*, means Madam Lisa. Lisa di Gherardini was twenty-six years old at the time the painting was made and had recently lost a child. That would explain her dark clothing and black veil, for these were the clothes people wore when they were in mourning.

There are other theories of the woman's identity. Some say it is Pacifica Brandano, a friend of Giuliano de' Medici. Some say it is Isabella, Gian Sforza's wife. Some think it is a portrait of Leonardo's beautiful mother. Some think she is too beautiful to be a real person and that she is an idealized woman. Others argue that she must be based on a real person because her features are so individual. Some art historians even claim that the *Mona Lisa* is a self-portrait of Leonardo, as if he were a young woman.

And what is she thinking? Why does she smile? A story is told that Leonardo had musicians and clowns in his bottega as the woman sat for her portrait, so that she would smile as he painted. But this smile has appeared in other paintings by Leonardo. Is he trying to tell us something? Is this a peaceful smile or is it a little disturbing? Why does she smile when she wears a black veil and all around her is dark and gloomy?

Leonardo took this painting with him everywhere. Some historians say it wasn't finished when Leonardo left Florence so he took it with him to complete it. If that is true, why didn't he send it to the person he painted it for when it was finished? Was there a problem with payment? Perhaps the woman died or the person who ordered the painting didn't want it anymore. Some say Leonardo fell in love with his own painting and couldn't give it up.

After Leonardo died, the painting was given to the king of France. In the late 1600s King Louis XIV moved it to his palace, Versailles. Louis XV didn't like the painting and had it hung in an out-of-the-way apartment of the palace. During the French Revolution it was hidden so it wouldn't be harmed. Napoleon kept it in his bedroom. Finally it was placed at the Louvre, a museum in Paris. During World War I and II it was sent out of the city for safekeeping. Only a couple of times has it been lent to museums in other countries.

It now hangs at the Louvre, heavily guarded and behind thick bullet-proof glass. Crowds of people come to see it every day. Songs have been written about it. One of the guards at the Louvre fell in love with *Mona Lisa* and became jealous of the people who came to look at her. In 1911, a man stole the painting from the Louvre and kept it in a trunk in his room in Paris for three years. When he tried to smuggle it into Italy he was caught and arrested and the painting was returned to France.

Whoever she is, Mona Lisa has captured the hearts of millions.

Mona Lisa,
Leonardo da
Vinci, 1503–05

Paintings can be appreciated just for the way they look. But you can enjoy a painting even more if you examine it and think about its meaning. When you look at a painting it is like having a conversation with the artist. Some artists are trying to make a moral point. Some want to show you the pure joy of color. Can you guess the message?

Take your time and make yourself comfortable. There's always a lot more to a painting than you see at first glance. Stand in front of the painting and let yourself get a feeling for it. Give it some time to work on your eyes, your mind, and your emotions.

What type of painting are you viewing? You might be looking at a landscape, a still life of fruit or flowers, or a portrait (like *Mona Lisa*). Can you tell if the painter used oil paints or watercolors? Can you see the brush strokes? Are figures outlined or did the artist use Leonardo's technique, sfumato? What is the composition of the painting? Look for shapes like circles and triangles.

Look for details. In the painting *Lady with Ermine* (see page 36), Leonardo painted Cecilia holding an ermine because that animal was a symbol of the Sforza family and Cecilia was a friend. Artists often use certain objects as symbols. In some older paintings dogs symbolized loyalty, water was a symbol of life, and skulls a symbol of death.

Color is used to make people feel emotion. What colors did the artist use and how do they make you feel? Sometimes color is used as a symbol or because it has become a tradition to paint certain things in a particular color. Blue is the traditional color for Mary's robe, and Leonardo followed that tradition in the *Virgin of the Rocks*. Look at the way the artist uses light. Light sets a mood and places the emphasis on certain figures and objects.

Think about the subject of the painting. Who do you think the people are? What are they doing? Is this a modern-day scene or one from many years ago? Where is it taking place? How are people dressed? Are they posing or just going about their activities? Think about why the artist chose this particular subject. He or she may be trying to make a point, but don't forget that sometimes artists are paid to paint specific things. If you know when the painting was made, read about the events of that time and think of how they might have influenced the artist.

Finally, write about the painting in your journal. Did you like the painting? Why or why not? How did it make you feel? What did it remind you of? Let your imagination go. Maybe it reminded you of a song or a person you know or a favorite book. What do you think the artist wants to say to you? Make up your own story or poem about the painting. Let it inspire you.

Detail from *Virgin of the Rocks*, Leonardo da Vinci, 1483–86

By the end of the year, Leonardo was once again reinstated in Milan as the court painter, engineer, and artistic advisor. It was almost as if he had returned to the happy times under Ludovico. He was able once again to pursue his interests in astronomy and mathematics. He studied with even greater enthusiasm the properties of water and tides and invented a device that measured the flow of water. Leonardo designed a dike and a long tunnel through a mountain. He studied the topography of the mountains.

Leonardo also returned to his research. By this time he had dissected approximately thirty bodies. He discovered arteriosclerosis by comparing the arteries and veins of a very old man and of a child. Now he concentrated on the study of muscles. He drew exact anatomical studies which would not be surpassed for centuries. Leonardo wanted to understand the development of the human organism from infancy through adulthood. He wanted to understand the origin of life.

He dissected the bodies of animals in order to compare them to human bodies. He studied plants and thought about how their parts were like the parts of the human body. In his geology notes, he referred to rivers as blood and soil as flesh and the rocky mountains as the bones of the earth. He wrote in his notes that "Man is the model of the world."

Anatomical sketches of the spine, Leonardo da Vinci, 1510

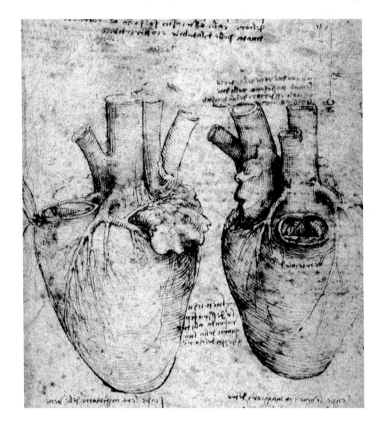

Anatomical study of heart, Leonardo da Vinci, 1513

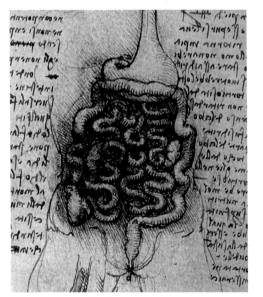

Anatomical study of intestines, Leonardo da Vinci, 1504–06

Opposite: Anatomical study of embryo in the womb, Leonardo da Vinci, 1510

Leonardo returned to his studies of flight and designed new flying machines. He studied the properties of clouds and rain. He also received a commission to make another bronze statue of a horse and rider, this time of one of the French generals.

In 1512 Ludovico's son, Maximilian, brought an army against the French and drove them out of Milan. Once again the Sforza family was in power. And once again without a patron, Leonardo decided to leave Milan. With Melzi and Salai, he spent a year in a small estate in the country. He was sixty-one years old, restless and anxious to get back to his work, but not sure where to go. He drew a portrait of himself in red chalk that shows the weariness he must have felt. Leonardo was an old man now, with a white beard and thick eyebrows.

The Medici family no longer ruled Florence, but had become a powerful force in Rome. One of Lorenzo's sons was named Pope. Another son, Giuliano, became commander in chief of the papal troops. In Rome, cathedrals were being built and artists were in demand. Giuliano found Leonardo and asked him to come to Rome. Giuliano became Leonardo's patron during his stay in this great city.

Though he was older now and failing in health, Leonardo stayed active and still passionately pursued his interests. The Vatican gardens were full of exotic plants and

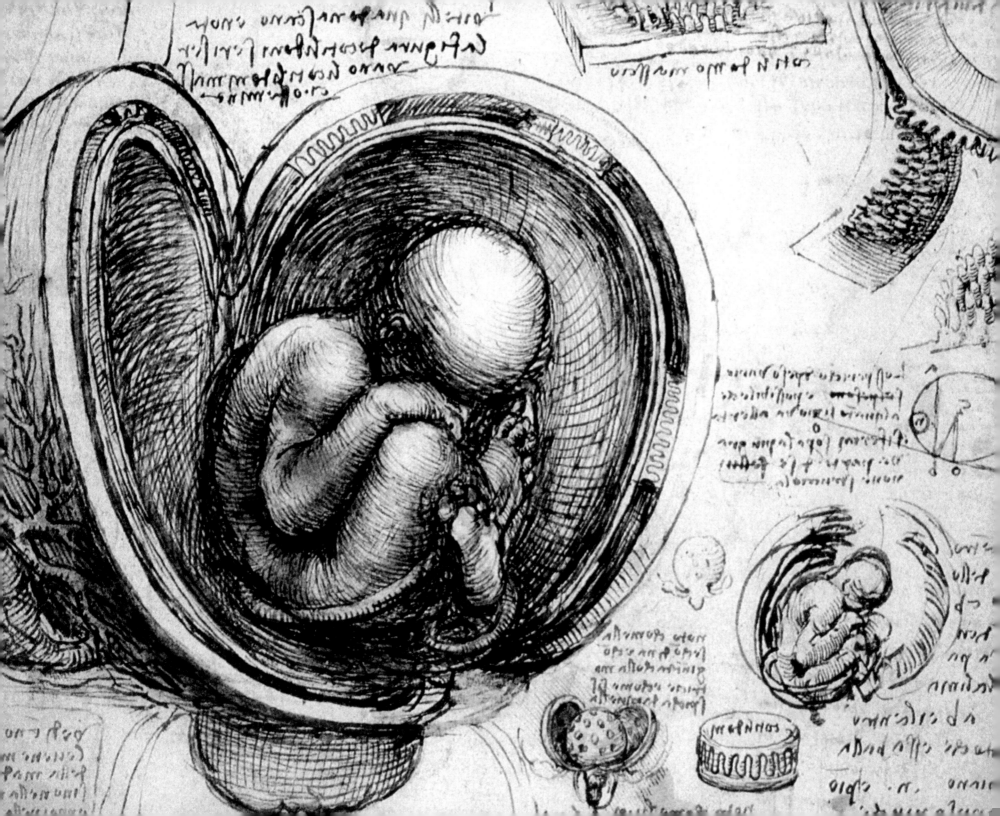

Leonardo used this time to study botany. He wrote a treatise on sound and the voice. He designed machines that could make rope and others to mint coins. He devised a plan to drain the marshes outside the city. He studied optics and built mirrors. He proposed using mirrors and solar power to produce energy to boil water for industry.

However, the years he spent in Rome were not happy times for him. He had two assistants who were lazy and who stole his ideas and sold them to others. One of the assistants accused him publicly of sorcery, and Leonardo was forbidden by the Pope to carry out his anatomical research.

Leonardo hated not being able to conduct his experiments and felt useless and unhappy. He stayed in his studio, writing long descriptions of catastrophic events and drawing sketches of deluges and storms. The war and destruction he had witnessed haunted him. Somehow during this difficult time he painted his last work, *St. John the Baptist*. He portrayed the saint smiling, almost like his *Mona Lisa*, and pointing up to heaven.

During this time a new king became the ruler of France. Francois I was eager to recapture Milan. In his first act as king he crossed the Alps and reconquered the city.

King Francois was a tall, handsome man with broad

St. John the Baptist, Leonardo da Vinci, 1513–16

As a boy, Leonardo studied the medicinal herbs that grew in Vinci. In Rome, he studied botany. He designed gardens for Charles d'Amboise and King Francois. You can grow an herb garden in your own kitchen.

Newspaper

Terra-cotta pots with drainage holes and saucers (or other containers such as a basket lined with thick plastic or a teacup and saucer)

Small pebbles

Trowel or large spoon

Potting soil

Seeds or seedlings (Get these at a nursery or gardening store. See suggestions below.)

Colored markers

Labels with sticky backing

Journal

Choose a spot for your plants—a sunny windowsill or a balcony—that receives at least 5 hours of direct sunlight every day. Spread newspaper out on the floor for a work space. Prepare the pots by lining the bottoms with a $1/2$–inch layer of small pebbles. Fill with potting soil.

The directions that came with your seeds and seedlings will tell you how deep and how far apart to plant them. They'll also tell when to expect seeds to sprout and how often to water. Most herbs like moist soil (but not soggy). Use your markers to make decorative labels showing the plant and its name. Attach them to the pots to identify your plants.

Keep a gardening journal, noting the date you planted and the date your seeds sprout. Draw pictures of the plants as they grow. Learn their Latin names. Notice how each plant has different leaves, flowers, and seeds.

To keep your plants full and bushy, trim them occasionally. Harvest them before they flower. For herbs with large leaves (like basil), cut the leaves from the stems and wash them in cold water. Spread them out on newspaper and leave them in a dark, dry room to dry. For herbs with small leaves, tie whole stems together and hang them upside down in a dark, dry place. When the leaves are dry and crisp, crush them into flakes and store them in clean jars. Be sure to label each jar including the name and date. Your herbs can keep up to one year.

Recommended herbs to plant are rosemary, sage, thyme, basil, oregano, lavender, bay, mint, anise, and summer savory.

shoulders. He also had a generous heart. He didn't imprison Maximilian Sforza but kept him at his court as a friend. Francois loved philosophy and science and art. He heard about Leonardo and wanted very much to meet him.

They did meet, during peace talks held between Rome and France. As a tribute to the ruler, Leonardo created a mechanical lion. During the opening ceremonies the lion walked up to the King on its spring-powered legs, then stopped. Hidden doors on its chest opened to show the French symbol of the lily, the fleur-de-lis. Francois was delighted and asked Leonardo to come to France to be his artist in residence.

In the summer of 1516 Leonardo accepted Francois's offer to join him. On his way out of Italy he visited Florence and Milan, taking three months to say goodbye to his country and his friends. He had with him trunks full of notebooks and supplies, and three paintings—*Mona Lisa, St. John the Baptist,* and *The Virgin and Child with Saint Anne.* Leonardo knew he'd never return to Italy. He settled in the Loire Valley, in a country house at Cloux, a short walk from the royal chateau. He became First Painter and Architect and Engineer of the King.

The king gave him acres of land with gardens and a vineyard, a fishing stream, and many trees. Leonardo, Melzi, and Salai lived in a house made of brick and white stone, with great stone fireplaces and many windows. The king visited Leonardo often and loved to talk with him about philosophy. Leonardo designed a town for the king with a royal chateau, elaborate gardens, canals, fountains, lakes, and parks. He was now paralyzed in one arm and no longer able to paint, but he could still draw and supervise the work of his pupil, Melzi. Leonardo wrote in his notebooks, "I shall continue." He never gave up his studies and his work.

One day the Cardinal of Aragon came to visit Leonardo. His secretary, Antonio, recorded the events of the day. Leonardo showed them his paintings. He showed them his notebooks on anatomy and painting and his volumes on the nature of water, along with many of his mechanical designs. He had often written in his notebooks the words, "Dimmi se mai fu fatto alcuma cosa?" ("Tell me if anything was accomplished.") But in the eyes of his visitors, his accomplishments were amazing.

In his sixty-seventh year, Leonardo drew up a will. He knew he was ill and dying. To Salai he left money and land, as he did for his half-brothers and his servants. To Francesco Melzi he left all of his books and writings and paintings. On May 2, 1519, Leonardo da Vinci died in the arms of King Francois.

The water you touch in a river is the last of that which has passed, and the first of that which is coming. Thus it is with time present.

—Leonardo

Self-Portrait, Leonardo da Vinci, 1512

Abacus: A tool for performing calculations by sliding counters along rods.

Altarpiece: A religious painting made for the altar of a church.

Alloy: A mixture of at least one metal with another substance.

Anatomy: The study of human and animal bodies.

Annunciation: The occasion when Mary learned from the angel Gabriel that she would bear the child of God.

Apprenticeship: A training period during which young people were committed to years of instruction under a master craftsman or merchant. The student, or apprentice, exchanged work for training in a trade or craft.

Bottega: A workshop or studio.

Cast: Making a statue by pouring liquid (such as molten metal or plaster) into a mold and letting it harden.

Chiaroscuro: An Italian word for bright and dark referring to the use of contrasting light and shadow in a painting.

City-State: See the sidebar on page 44.

Commission: In art, a formal agreement to create a specific work.

Composition: The arrangement of figures in a painting.

Classic, classical: Greek or Roman art of ancient times. This art was known for its symmetry and harmony.

Fresco: The word for "fresh" in Italian. In art, it means the technique of applying water-based paint to damp plaster. The painting then becomes part of the wall's permanent surface. Fresco is used to describe both the technique and the painting.

Gothic buildings: Medieval architecture from the years 1200–1500 noted for pointed towers and peaked arches.

Guild: People in various trades grouped together in associations, or guilds. These groups determined the rules for their trades and set prices for their services.

Lute: A stringed musical instrument.

Masque: A masquerade or party. Party goers dressed in costumes and performed plays and dances.

Medium: The material an artist uses to make a work of art, such as paint, clay, stone, or wood.

Monastery: A building that serves as the home for a community of monks.

Oil paint: Oil paints were introduced into Italy from northern Europe in the middle of the fifteenth century. They were made of powdered pigments, or colors, that were mixed with linseed oil.

Patron: A wealthy sponsor of an artist; a person who supported the artist so that he or she could work without concern for his or her livelihood.

Anatomical study of hands, Leonardo da Vinci, 1510

Perspective: The technique used by artists so that objects in paintings appear to have depth and solidity.

Pigment: A powdered substance that, mixed with liquid, gives color.

Pope: The head of the Roman Catholic Church.

Portrait: A painting of a particular person.

Proportion: The relationship between the size of a figure and the size of its parts.

Regent: A person governing a kingdom in the place of a ruler who is a minor or is otherwise unable to rule.

Renaissance: See the sidebar on page 18.

Scale: Relative size. A length used to represent a larger unit of measure (for example, one inch equaling one mile).

Sculpture: The act of carving, cutting, or casting materials into a statue; the statue itself is also referred to as sculpture.

Self-portrait: A drawing or painting by the artist of himself or herself.

Sfumato: "Smoky" in Italian, sfumato is a technique Leonardo used that showed softened outlines and blurred shadows.

Tempera: A paint made of powdered pigments mixed with egg yolks. This was a popular paint in the fifteenth century.

Three-dimensional: Having height, width, and depth.

Two-dimensional: Having only height and width.

Vanishing point: A single point in a picture where all parallel lines seem to meet.

Villa: A country house and estate.

RENAISSANCE ARTISTS

Botticelli (1444–1510) was one of the most important artists of his time. Born to a modest family in Florence, Sandro Botticelli was a poor student so his father apprenticed him to a goldsmith. He studied painting under the master Fillippo Lippi, but he was greatly influenced by Verrocchio. Eventually, he became a favorite of the wealthy Medici family; Botticelli was one of the many artists who worked on the Vatican in Rome. In 1495 he became a follower of the preacher Savonarola, who condemned the way wealthy people lived. Under Savonarola's influence Botticelli reportedly burned many of his paintings. Fortunately, many other beautiful and poetic paintings of his remain so that we may enjoy them today. Botticelli is known as a master of line. This means that the figures in his paintings are precisely drawn but they also have a dreamy quality about them. You can see one of his masterpieces, *Adoration of the Magi*, on page 19.

Giotto (1266–1337) was a Florentine painter, architect, and sculptor. For many art historians he represents the beginning of Italian painting; some also say he is the first modern artist. Giotto was a master of design and composition. He created powerful and original paintings with lifelike figures. He was influenced by the painter Cimabue and spent his early years in Rome. He also worked in Naples but came back to Florence to work on that city's cathedral.

Masaccio (1402–1428) was a Florentine painter who, at the age of twenty-one, single-handedly launched a new style in art with his use of scientific perspective in painting. His carefully composed frescoes greatly influenced Leonardo da Vinci and many other Renaissance artists. Not much is known about Masaccio's early years. Once, he was a member of the physicians' guild. He had a very brief career as an artist and died when he was only twenty-seven. A detail from his painting *Expulsion of Adam and Eve* can be seen on page 18.

Michelangelo (1475–1564) was an Italian sculptor, painter, architect, and poet who was Leonardo da Vinci's greatest rival. Born Michelangelo Buonarroti in Caprese, he was the son of a minor official. He moved to Florence as a child and was briefly apprenticed to the artist Ghirlandio, then he moved to the workshop of the sculptor Bertoldo in the Medici garden. From his early years, he was most drawn to sculpture; his love for it and for the human form is reflected in his paintings. After his patron Lorenzo Medici died, Michelangelo moved to Rome, where he worked on the tomb for Pope Julius II and painted the ceiling frescoes of the Sistine Chapel. Among the

Study of arms and hands, Leonardo da Vinci, 1474

sculptures of this inspired genius are *David*, a heroic youth, and the *Pieta*, a figure of Christ on the lap of his mother. He also completed the dome of St. Peter's church in Rome. Michelangelo's works are known for their exceptional beauty and power. He was the most renowned artist of his time and probably the greatest sculptor of all time. A detail from his painting *The Holy Family* can be seen on page 19.

Perugino (1446–1524) was one of the painters who decorated the walls of the Sistine Chapel. This Roman artist was born Pietro Vannucci, but took his name Perugino from the town of his birth, Perugia. He was a student in Verrocchio's workshop and became the teacher of the great artist Raphael. Perugino's frescoes, portraits, and altarpieces are known for their sweetness and harmony. Turn to page 16 to see his painting *Christ Giving the Keys to St. Peter* and note its perfect balance and solidity.

Raphael (1483–1520) is considered the central painter of the Renaissance. His paintings have come to define the era. Born Raffaello Sanzio in Urbino, he was the son of a painter. He trained under Perugino and quickly surpassed his teacher. He was greatly influenced by Leonardo da Vinci and Michelangelo; in his painting *The School of Athens*, he used Leonardo as one of his models. He was called to Rome to work on the Vatican and became a hugely successful

artist who lived, it is said, "more like a prince than a painter." A detail from his painting *St. Michael Victorious* is on page 18 and you can see his painting *Marriage of the Virgin* on page 19.

Titian (1477–1576) was born in the town of Cadore and as a young boy he moved to Venice to study under a painter and mosaic artist named Sebastiano Zuccato. Venetian artists were known for their use of color and Titian became the master of color. His works are rich and very expressive. Titian, who lived to be nearly 100 years old, revolutionized painting. His influence on other artists was enormous; he is one of the most important artists in history. A detail from his work *Sacred and Profane Love* can be seen on page 19.

Verrocchio (1435–1488) was an Italian painter, goldsmith, and sculptor. He is best known as Leonardo da Vinci's teacher but he was one of the finest and most successful artists in Florence during that city's greatest era. The son of a brickmaker, Verrocchio was born Andrea di Michele di Francesco Ciono, but he called himself Verrocchio after his teacher, Giuliano da Verrochi. At that time, adopting your teacher's name was customary. He went on to become one of the most important Renaissance sculptors and the teacher of some of the greatest artists of the Renaissance. You can see his sculpture *David* on page 12.

HISTORICAL FIGURES

Cesare Borgia (1476–1507), the Duke of Valentinois, was an adventurer, a ruthless soldier and military leader, and a cardinal. He attempted to conquer central Italy but failed. He left Italy and was eventually killed in battle. Machiavelli's book *The Prince* is said to be based on his observations of Cesare Borgia.

Christopher Columbus (1446–1506) was an Italian navigator who sailed across the Atlantic Ocean and discovered America in 1492. Spain's King Ferdinand and Queen Isabella financed his voyages to the Far East. Columbus never fulfilled his dream of reaching the Far East by sailing west; but his discovery of the new world changed the course of history.

Nicolaus Copernicus (1473–1543) was a Polish astronomer who developed the theory that the earth and other planets revolve around the sun. Copernicus taught his theories in Italy.

Isabella d'Este (1474–1539), the Marchioness of Mantua, was from an aristocratic Italian family. Her brother was a cardinal. She was a patroness of the arts who collected the works of many artists, including Leonardo da Vinci.

Francois I (1494–1547) was the King of France from 1515 until his death. He was a great lover of art who brought

Leonardo da Vinci to France, supported Raphael, and was painted by Titian.

Vasco da Gama (1469–1524) was a Portuguese navigator who in 1498 discovered the route from Portugal to India by sailing around Africa. His four ships returned to Portugal the following year, loaded with spices and other goods from the Far East.

Johannes Gutenberg (1398–1468) was a German printer who invented movable type in 1438 and used it to publish the Bible. His real name was Johannes Gutenberg Gensfleisch but he preferred to use his middle name (his last name means *gooseflesh* in German).

Louis XII (1462–1515), known as "The Father of the People," was the king of France from 1498 to 1515. He was the son of Charles d'Orleans and founder of the line of Valois–Orleans.

Martin Luther (1483–1546) was a German monk and scholar who in 1517 challenged the established church by nailing his written protests to the doors of the Wittenberg cathedral. His actions started the Protestant Reformation and changed the course of history.

Niccolo di Bernardo Machiavelli (1469–1527) was an Italian statesman. He wrote about government and power in a book called *The Prince*, which was based on his close observations of the ruthless Cesare Borgia and other powerful men of that time.

Ferdinand Magellan (1480–1521) was a Portuguese navigator who set out from Spain with five ships. He sought and found a passage around South America and crossed the Pacific Ocean to discover the Philippine Islands. He was killed there but his crews continued their voyage—the first voyage around the world.

Lorenzo Medici (1449–1492) was known as Lorenzo the Magnificent. He was a rich and powerful statesman and the ruler of Florence. Lorenzo took over the rule of Florence when he was only twenty years old. Florence and its artists prospered under his patronage. Lorenzo was also a poet and a passionate collector of beautiful things.

Ludovico Sforza (1451–1508) was the Duke of Milan for only five years, from 1494 to 1500, but he ruled the city in his nephew's name for many years. This wealthy patron of Leonardo's was the son and grandson of powerful Italian mercenaries, or hired military chiefs. Their castle, the Castello Sforzesco, still stands in Milan. It is now a museum that houses many important historical and art objects.

WEB SITES TO EXPLORE

Art and History

Exploring Leonardo

http://www.mos.org/sln/Leonardo/LeoHomePage.html

This is a web page from the Museum of Science in Boston.

Galleria degli Uffizi in Florence

http://www.uffizi.firenze.it

This web page is from the Uffizi Gallery in Florence.

The Leonardo Museum in Vinci

http://www.leonet.it/comuni/vincimus/invinmus.html

The Louvre

http://mistral.culture.fr/louvre/

Here you can view the treasures of the Louvre museum in Paris.

National Gallery of Art

http://www.nga.gov

See the treasures of the National Gallery at this web site.

Virtual Renaissance

http://www.twingroves.district96.k12.il.us/Renaissance/VirtualRen.html

Historical figures take you on a tour of the Renaissance.

Science

American Birding Association

http://www.americanbirding.org/

Learn about our feathered friends at this site.

Ask Dr. Math

http://forum.swarthmore.edu/dr.math/

Get your math answers here.

Bill Nye, The Science Guy

http://nyelabs.kcts.org/

A great site for lots of fun and science.

Human Anatomy On-line

http://www.innerbody.com/indexbody.html

This site contains over 100 illustrations of the human body.

Institute and Museum of History of Science

http://galileo.imss.firenze.it/

The Florence Museum's web page.

Detail of *Bust of a Warrior*, Leonardo da Vinci, 1477

Leonardo da Vinci National Museum of Science and Technology in Milan

http://www.museoscienza.org/english/leonardo/

Choose a character and walk (or fly!) through this virtual museum of Leonardo's inventions.

Simple Machines

http://wildcats.lafsd.k12.ca.us/stanley/projects/simp1.html

Examples of simple machines and how they work

Smithsonian Institute

http://www.si.edu/newstart.html

This site is filled with interesting science.

To Fly Is Everything

http://hawaii.cogsci.uiuc.edu/invent/air_main.shtml

This is a virtual museum of the airplane.

WHERE TO SEE LEONARDO DA VINCI'S WORKS

Baptism of Christ (with Verrocchio)
Galleria degli Uffizi, Florence, Italy

The Annunciation
Galleria degli Uffizi, Florence, Italy

Portrait of Ginevra
National Gallery of Art, Washington D.C., United States

Adoration of the Magi
Galleria degli Uffizi, Florence, Italy

St. Jerome
Vatican Museum, Rome, Italy

Virgin of the Rocks
Louvre, Paris, France

Lady with Ermine
Czartoryski Museum, Cracow, Poland

The Last Supper
Santa Maria delle Grazie, Milan, Italy

Mona Lisa
Louvre, Paris, France

Study for Virgin and Child with St. Anne
National Gallery, London, England

Self-Portrait
Biblioteca Reale, Turin, Italy

St. John the Baptist
Louvre, Paris, France

The Windsor Castle Royal Library holds hundreds of sketches by Leonardo.

The National Museum of Science and Technology in Milan has a floor dedicated to Leonardo's inventions.

In Vinci, Italy, a whole museum is devoted to him—The Leonardo da Vinci Museum.

Bramly, Serge. *Leonardo: Discovering the Life of Leonardo da Vinci.* New York: Edward Burlingame Books/Harper-Collins Publishers, 1991.

Brown, David. *Leonardo's Last Supper: The Restoration.* Washington, D.C.: National Gallery of Art catalog, 1983.

Cole, Alison. *Eyewitness Art: The Renaissance.* London: Dorling Kindersley, 1994.

Dioguardi, Raffaele, ed. *NTC's Beginner's Italian and English Dictionary.* Lincolnwood, Illinois: NTC Publishing Group, 1995.

Fradon, Dana. *Harold the Herald: A Book About Heraldry.* New York: Dutton Books, 1990.

Horton, James. *The DK Art School: An Introduction to Drawing.* London: Dorling Kindersley, 1994.

Howarth, Sarah. *Renaissance People.* Brookfield, Connecticut: The Millbrook Press, 1992.

Janson, H. W. and Anthony Janson. *History of Art for Young People.* New York: Harry N. Abrams, Inc., 1997.

Macaulay, David. *The Way Things Work.* Boston: Houghton Mifflin Company, 1988.

MacCurdy, Edward. *The Notebooks of Leonardo da Vinci.* New York: George Braziller, 1954.

Muhlberger, Richard. *What Makes a Leonardo a Leonardo?* New York: The Metropolitan Museum of Art and Viking, 1994.

Powell, Anton. *Modern Knowledge Library: Renaissance Italy.* New York: Warwick Press, 1980.

Reit, Seymour. *The Day They Stole the Mona Lisa.* Arlington, Texas: Summit Books, 1981.

Romei, Francesca. *Masters of Art: Leonardo da Vinci.* New York: Peter Bedrick Books, 1994.

Rupp, Rebecca. *Everything You Never Learned About Birds.* Pownal, Vermont: Storey Communications, Inc., 1995.

Travis, David. *The Land and People of Italy.* New York: HarperCollins Publishers, 1992.

Vasari, Giorgio. *The Lives of the Artists.* New York: Penguin Books, 1965.

Waters, Elizabeth and Annie Harris. *Painting: A Young Artist's Guide.* London: Dorling Kindersley, 1993.

Wolfflin, Heinrich. *Classical Art: An Introduction to the Italian Renaissance.* London: Phaidon Press, 1994.

Wood, Robert W. *Science for Kids: 39 Easy Geography Activities.* Blue Ridge Summit, Pennsylvania: TAB Books, 1992.

Woolf, Felicity. *Picture This: A First Introduction to Paintings.* New York: Doubleday, 1990.

Yanawine, Philip. *Key Art Terms for Beginners.* New York: Harry N. Abrams, Inc., 1995.

Detail of deluge, Leonardo da Vinci, 1514

Page

ii *Mona Lisa*, Leonardo da Vinci, 1503–05. Courtesy of Wood River Gallery

Ground plan for a basilica, Leonardo da Vinci, 1490. Courtesy of Wood River Gallery

iii Detail from *Lady with Ermine*, Leonardo da Vinci, 1483–88. Courtesy of Wood River Gallery

Detail from *Baptism of Christ*, Andrea del Verrocchio and Leonardo da Vinci, 1472–75. Courtesy of Wood River Gallery

Sketch of parts of a machine, Leonardo da Vinci, 1480. Courtesy of Wood River Gallery

vi Diagram of human proportions, Leonardo da Vinci, 1492. Courtesy of Wood River Gallery

xii Study for the head of Leda, Leonardo da Vinci, 1505–07. Courtesy of Planet Art

1 Detail from study for a Madonna and child, Leonardo da Vinci. 1478. Courtesy of Planet Art

6 Detail from *Baptism of Christ*, Andrea del Verrocchio and Leonardo da Vinci, 1472–75. Courtesy of Wood River Gallery

7 Detail from *Adoration of the Magi*, Leonardo da Vinci, 1481–82. Courtesy of Wood River Gallery

9 *Portrait of a Musician*, Leonardo da Vinci, 1490. Courtesy of Planet Art

12 Statue of David, Andrea del Verrocchio, 1476. Courtesy of Erich Lessing/Art Resource, NY

14 Top: Detail from *The Tribute Money*, Masacchio, 1427. Courtesy of Planet Art

Bottom: Detail of *Madonna Enthroned* (front of Maestra Altar), Duccio, 1308–11. Courtesy of Planet Art

16 Top: Detail from *The Month of August in The Book of Hours*, The Limbourg Brothers, 1413–16. Courtesy of Planet Art

Bottom: *Christ Giving Keys to St. Peter*, Perugino, 1481. Courtesy of Planet Art

17 Detail from *Madonna with Child and Vase of Flowers*, Leonardo da Vinci, late 1470's. Courtesy of Planet Art

18 Top: Detail from *Expulsion of Adam and Eve*, Masaccio, 1425–28. Courtesy of Planet Art

Bottom: Detail from *St. Michael Victorious*, Raphael, 1518. Courtesy of Planet Art

19 Top left: Detail from *Adoration of the Magi*, Botticelli, 1475. Courtesy of Planet Art

Top right: Detail from *Marriage of the Virgin*, Raphael, 1504. Courtesy of Planet Art

Detail from drawing for *Leda and the Swan*, Leonardo da Vinci, 1505–07

Bottom left: Detail from *Sacred and Profane Love*, Titian, 1514. Courtesy of Planet Art

Bottom right: Detail from *The Holy Family*, Michelangelo, 1503. Courtesy of Planet Art

22 Detail from *Baptism of Christ*, Andrea del Verrocchio and Leonardo da Vinci, 1472–75. Courtesy of Wood River Gallery

23 *The Annunciation*, Leonardo da Vinci, 1473–75. Courtesy of Wood River Gallery

26 *Adoration of the Magi*, Leonardo da Vinci, 1481–82. Courtesy of Wood River Gallery

27 Drawing for a city on two levels, Leonardo da Vinci, early 1490s. Courtesy of Planet Art

28 Detail from *The Benois Madonna*, Leonardo da Vinci, 1480. Courtesy of Planet Art

29 Diagram of human proportions, Leonardo da Vinci, 1492. Courtesy Wood River Gallery

30 *Angel with Lute*, Associate of Leonardo da Vinci, 1490s. Courtesy of Wood River Gallery

32 Study of the hand and arm, Leonardo da Vinci, 1510. Courtesy of Planet Art

34 Anatomical study of a woman's body, Leonardo da Vinci, 1506–08. Courtesy of Planet Art

36 *Lady with Ermine*, Leonardo da Vinci, 1485. Courtesy of Wood River Gallery

37 *Virgin of the Rocks*, Leonardo da Vinci, 1483–86. Courtesy Erich Lessing/Art Resource, NY

38 Anatomical study of skull, Leonardo da Vinci, 1489. Courtesy of Planet Art

39 Drawing for a city on two levels, Leonardo da Vinci, early 1490s. Courtesy of Planet Art

43 Top: Sketch of parts of a machine, Leonardo da Vinci, 1480. Courtesy Wood River Gallery

Bottom: Sketch of treadmill crossbow, Leonardo da Vinci, 1488. Courtesy Wood River Gallery

44 Top: Detail from a map of Florence. Courtesy of Planet Art

Bottom: Map of Italy, 1600. Courtesy of Planet Art

45 Study for the head of St. Anne, Leonardo da Vinci, 1508–10. Courtesy of Wood River Gallery

48 Study of cats and dragon, Leonardo da Vinci, 1513–14. Courtesy of Planet Art

50 Sketch of human proportions, Leonardo da Vinci, 1488–89. Courtesy of Planet Art

51 Study for the dome of the Milan cathedral, Leonardo da Vinci, 1488. Courtesy of Planet Art

52 Studies for a domed church, Leonardo da Vinci, 1485–90. Courtesy of Planet Art

54 Diagram of a flying machine, Leonardo da Vinci, 1486–90. Courtesy of Wood River Gallery

56 *The Last Supper*, Leonardo da Vinci, 1495–98. Courtesy of Scala/Art Resource, NY

57 Top left: Study for *The Last Supper*, Leonardo da Vinci, 1497. Courtesy of Planet Art

Top right: Study for *The Battle of Anghiari*, Leonardo da Vinci, 1503–04. Courtesy of Planet Art

Bottom left: Old man with oak leaves and caricatures, Leonardo da Vinci, late 1490s. Courtesy of Planet Art

Bottom right: Study of an old man, Leonardo da Vinci, 1500. Courtesy of Planet Art

58 Detail from *The Last Supper*, Leonardo da Vinci, 1495–98. Courtesy of Scala/Art Resource, NY

61 Study of an old man, Leonardo da Vinci, 1500. Courtesy of Planet Art

62 Drawing for *The Virgin and Child with Saint Anne*, Leonardo da Vinci, 1498. Courtesy of Wood River Gallery

63 Top: Sketch of Castello Sforzesco, Leonardo da Vinci, 1497. Courtesy of Planet Art

Bottom: Sketch of treadmill crossbow, Leonardo da Vinci, 1488. Courtesy of Planet Art

64 Detail of *Saint Jerome*, Leonardo da Vinci, 1480. Courtesy of Wood River Gallery

67 Drawing after Leonardo's *The Battle of Anghiari*, Peter Paul Rubens, 1605. Courtesy of Wood River Gallery

71 *Mona Lisa*, Leonardo da Vinci, 1503–05. Courtesy of Wood River Gallery

72 Detail of *Virgin of the Rocks*, Leonardo da Vinci, 1483–86. Courtesy of Erich Lessing/Art Resource, NY

73 Anatomical sketches of the spine, Leonardo da Vinci, 1510. Courtesy of Planet Art

74 Top: Anatomical study of the heart, Leonardo da Vinci, 1513. Courtesy of Planet Art

Bottom: Anatomical study of intestines, Leonardo da Vinci, 1504–06. Courtesy of Planet Art

75 Anatomical study of embryo in the womb, Leonardo da Vinci, 1510. Courtesy of Planet Art

76 *St. John the Baptist*, Leonardo da Vinci, 1513–16. Courtesy Erich Lessing/Art Resource, NY

79 *Self-Portrait*, Leonardo da Vinci, 1512. Courtesy of Wood River Gallery

80 Anatomical study of hands, Leonardo da Vinci, 1510. Courtesy of Planet Art

82 Study of arms and hands, Leonardo da Vinci, 1474. Courtesy of Planet Art

85 Detail of Bust of a Warrior, Leonardo da Vinci, 1477. Courtesy of Planet Art

87 Detail of deluge, Leonardo da Vinci, 1514. Courtesy of Planet Art

88 Detail from drawing for *Leda and the Swan*, Leonardo da Vinci, 1505–07. Courtesy of Planet Art

91 Detail of drapery study, Leonardo da Vinci, 1496. Courtesy of Planet Art

Detail of drapery study,
Leonardo da Vinci, 1496